GIORGIO GIACOSA

# WOMEN OF THE CAESARS

*Their Lives and Portraits on Coins*

TRANSLATION BY R. ROSS HOLLOWAY

EDIZIONI ARTE E MONETA, PUBLISHERS

Distributed in North America by
Abner Schram (Schram Enterprises Ltd.)
36 PARK ST.
MONTCLAIR, N.J., 07042
ISBN 0-8390-0193-2

# Index

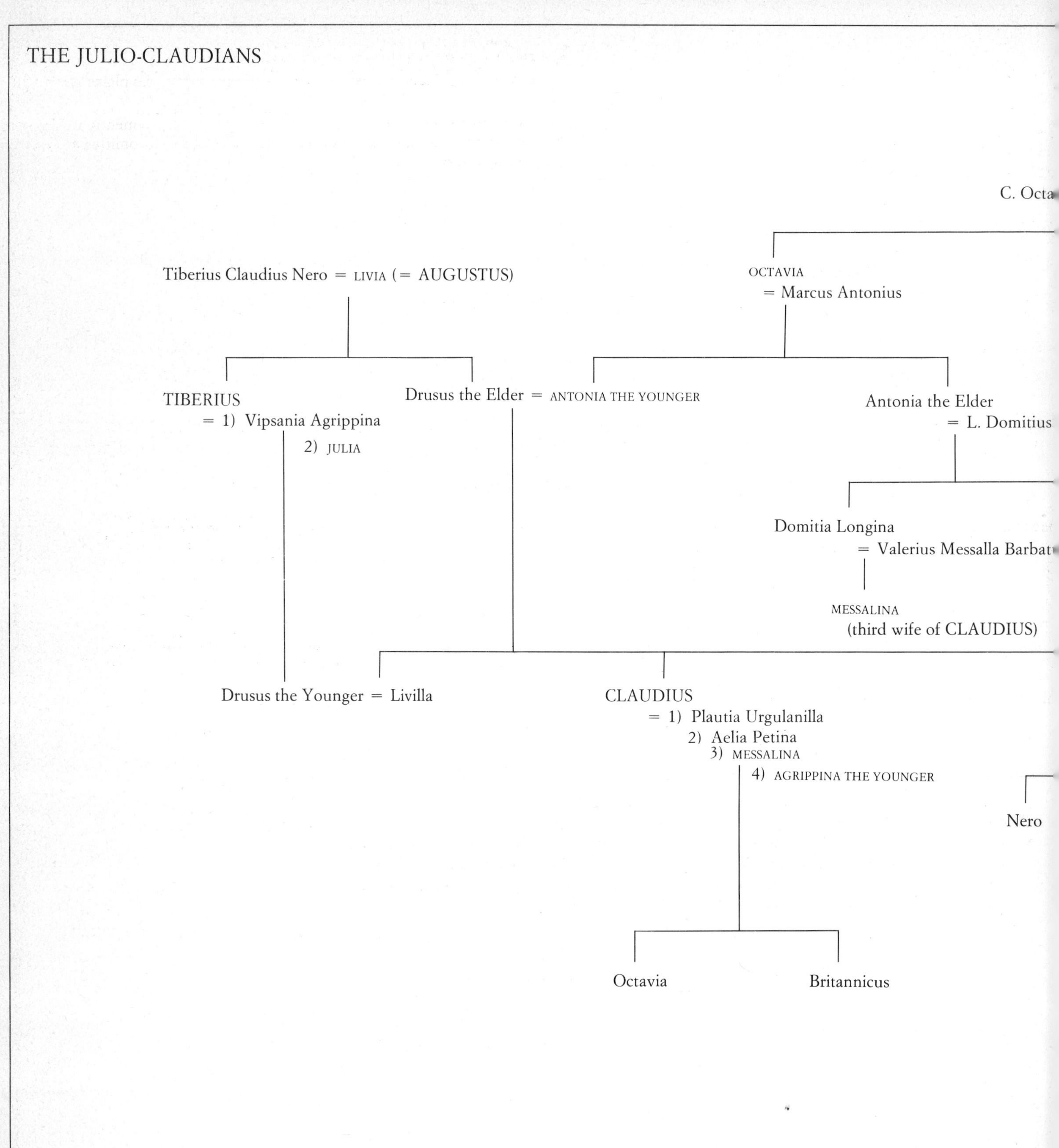
THE JULIO-CLAUDIANS
C. Octa
Tiberius Claudius Nero = LIVIA (= AUGUSTUS)
OCTAVIA
= Marcus Antonius
TIBERIUS
= 1) Vipsania Agrippina
2) JULIA
Drusus the Elder = ANTONIA THE YOUNGER
Antonia the Elder
= L. Domitius
Domitia Longina
= Valerius Messalla Barbat
MESSALINA
(third wife of CLAUDIUS)
Drusus the Younger = Livilla
CLAUDIUS
= 1) Plautia Urgulanilla
2) Aelia Petina
3) MESSALINA
4) AGRIPPINA THE YOUNGER
Nero
Octavia
Britannicus

The names of the emperors are written in capitals.

The names of the ladies whose portraits are illustrated on the plates are in red.

To ensure clarity, the names of some personages who, though mentioned in the text, do not have an important historical role have been omitted from the genealogical tree.

Atia

Octavianus AUGUSTUS
= 1) Scribonia
2) LIVIA

barbus

JULIA
= 1) Marcellus
2) Agrippa
3) TIBERIUS

naeus Domitius Ahenobarbus
= AGRIPPINA THE YOUNGER

nicus = AGRIPPINA THE ELDER

Gaius

Lucius

Julia

Agrippa Postumus

Drusus

CALIGULA
= 1) Junia Claudilla
2) Livia Orestilla
3) Lollia Paulina
4) Milonia Caesonia

AGRIPPINA THE YOUNGER
= 1) Gnaeus Domitius Ahenobarbus
2) C. Passienus Crispus
3) CLAUDIUS

NERO
= 1) Octavia
2) POPPAEA
3) Statilia Messalina

DRUSILLA

JULIA LIVILLA

# THE FLAVIANS

VESPASIANUS
= DOMITILLA

Flavia Domitilla

TITUS
= Marcia Furnilla

JULIA
= Titus Flavius Sabinus
later mistress of DOMITIANUS

DOMITIANUS
= DOMITIA LONGINA

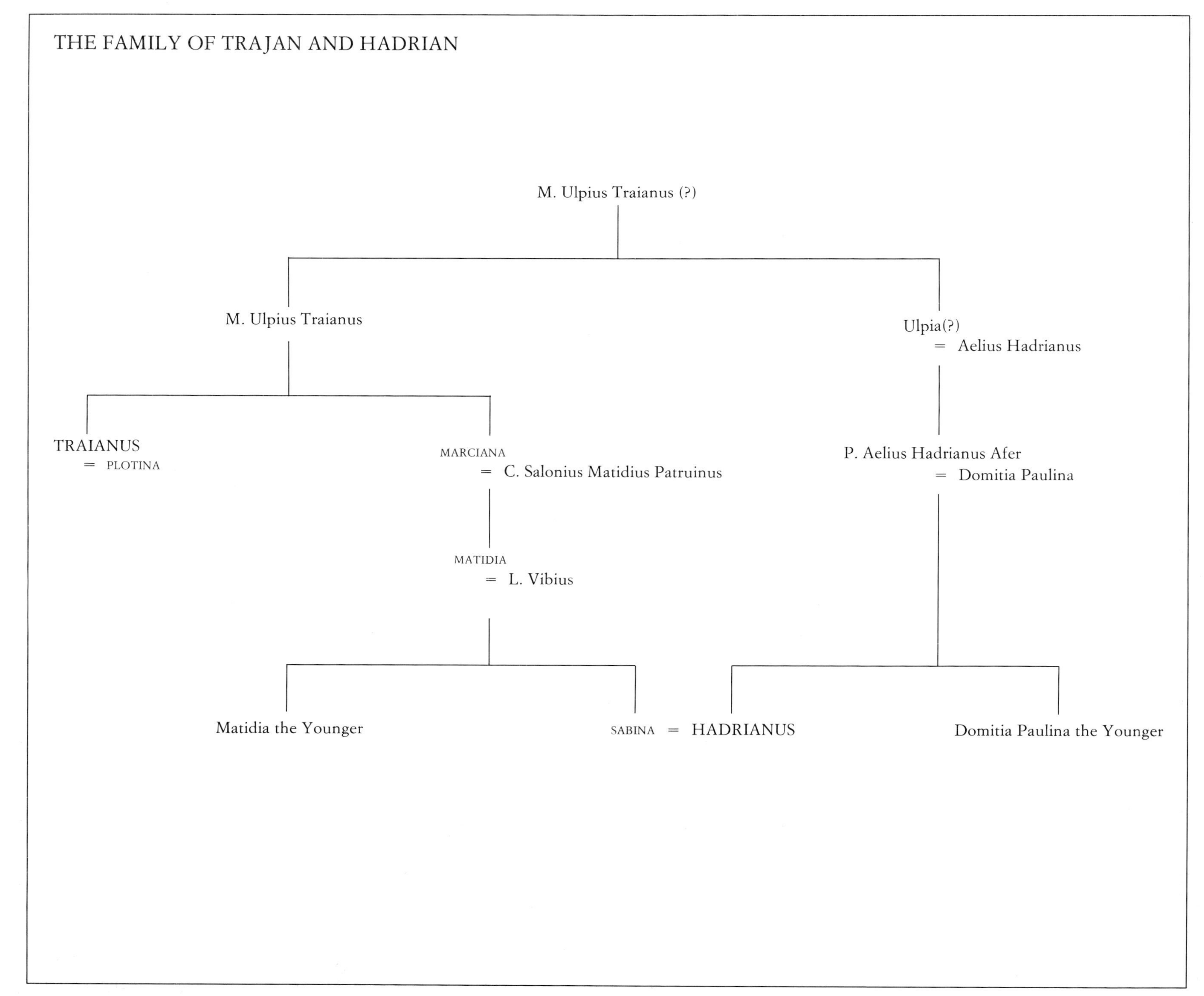
THE FAMILY OF TRAJAN AND HADRIAN
M. Ulpius Traianus (?)
M. Ulpius Traianus
Ulpia(?)
= Aelius Hadrianus
TRAIANUS
= PLOTINA
MARCIANA
= C. Salonius Matidius Patruinus
P. Aelius Hadrianus Afer
= Domitia Paulina
MATIDIA
= L. Vibius
Matidia the Younger
SABINA = HADRIANUS
Domitia Paulina the Younger

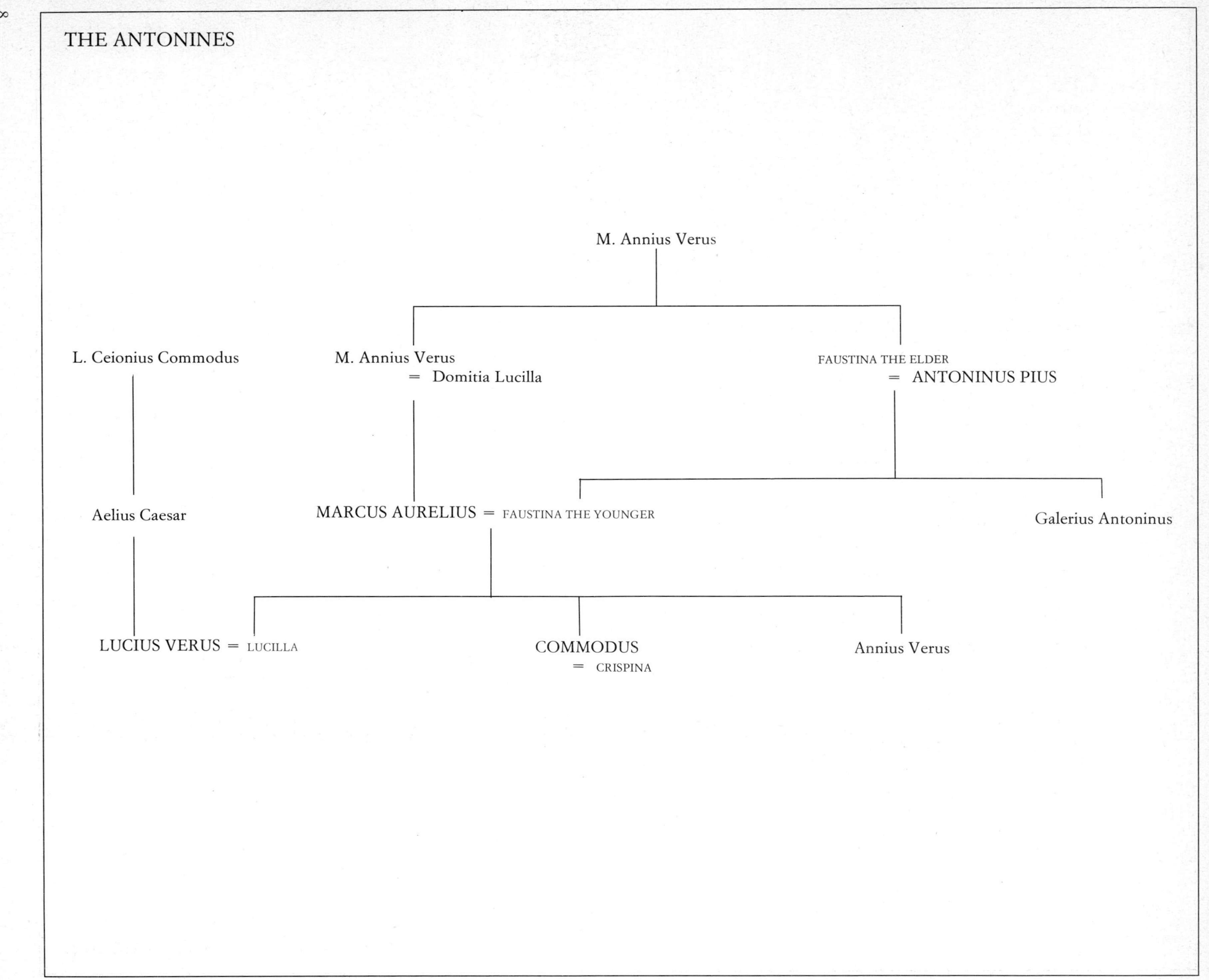
THE ANTONINES
M. Annius Verus
L. Ceionius Commodus
M. Annius Verus = Domitia Lucilla
FAUSTINA THE ELDER = ANTONINUS PIUS
Aelius Caesar
MARCUS AURELIUS = FAUSTINA THE YOUNGER
Galerius Antoninus
LUCIUS VERUS = LUCILLA
COMMODUS = CRISPINA
Annius Verus

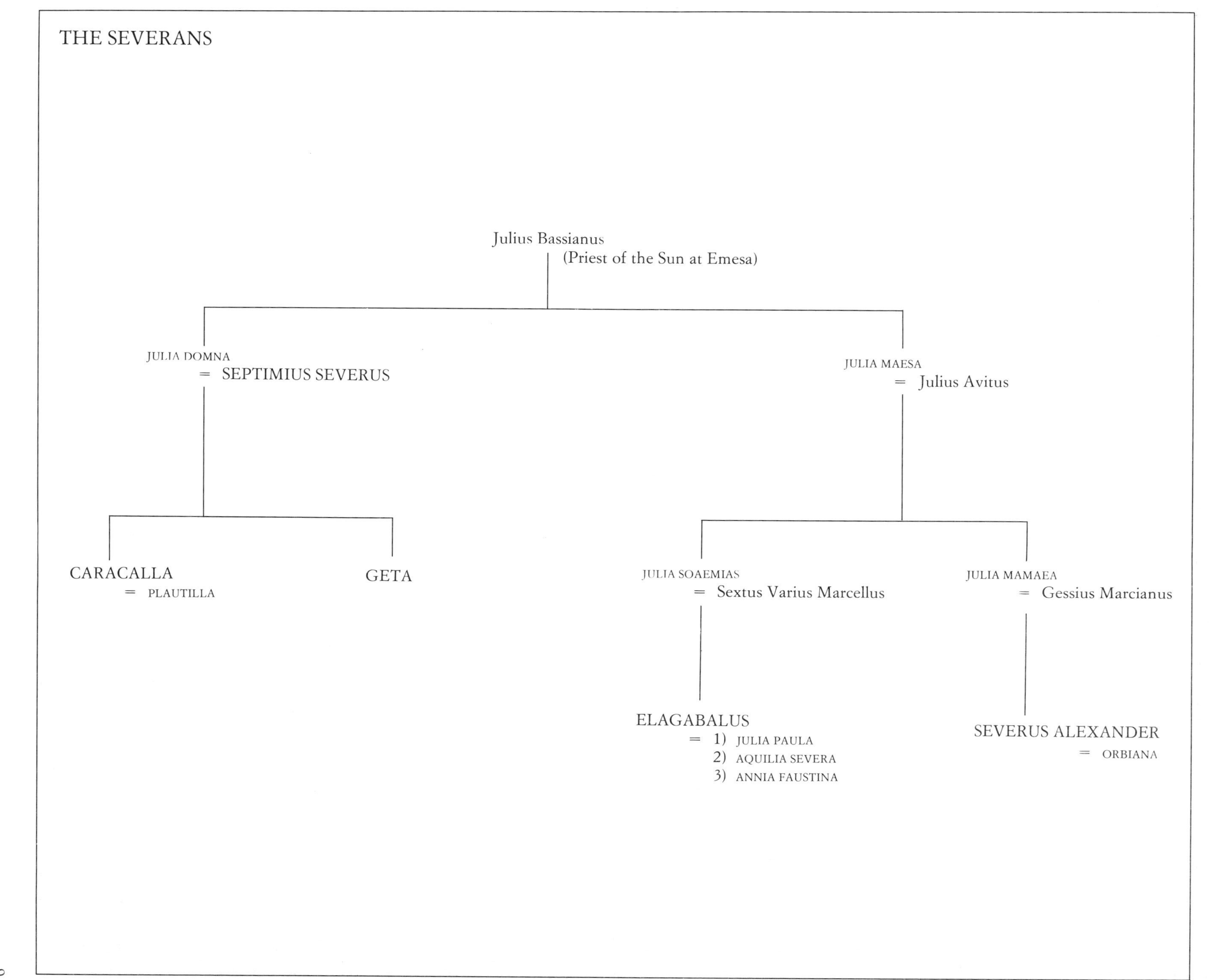

THE SEVERANS
Julius Bassianus
(Priest of the Sun at Emesa)
JULIA DOMNA
= SEPTIMIUS SEVERUS
JULIA MAESA
= Julius Avitus
CARACALLA
= PLAUTILLA
GETA
JULIA SOAEMIAS
= Sextus Varius Marcellus
JULIA MAMAEA
= Gessius Marcianus
ELAGABALUS
= 1) JULIA PAULA
2) AQUILIA SEVERA
3) ANNIA FAUSTINA
SEVERUS ALEXANDER
= ORBIANA

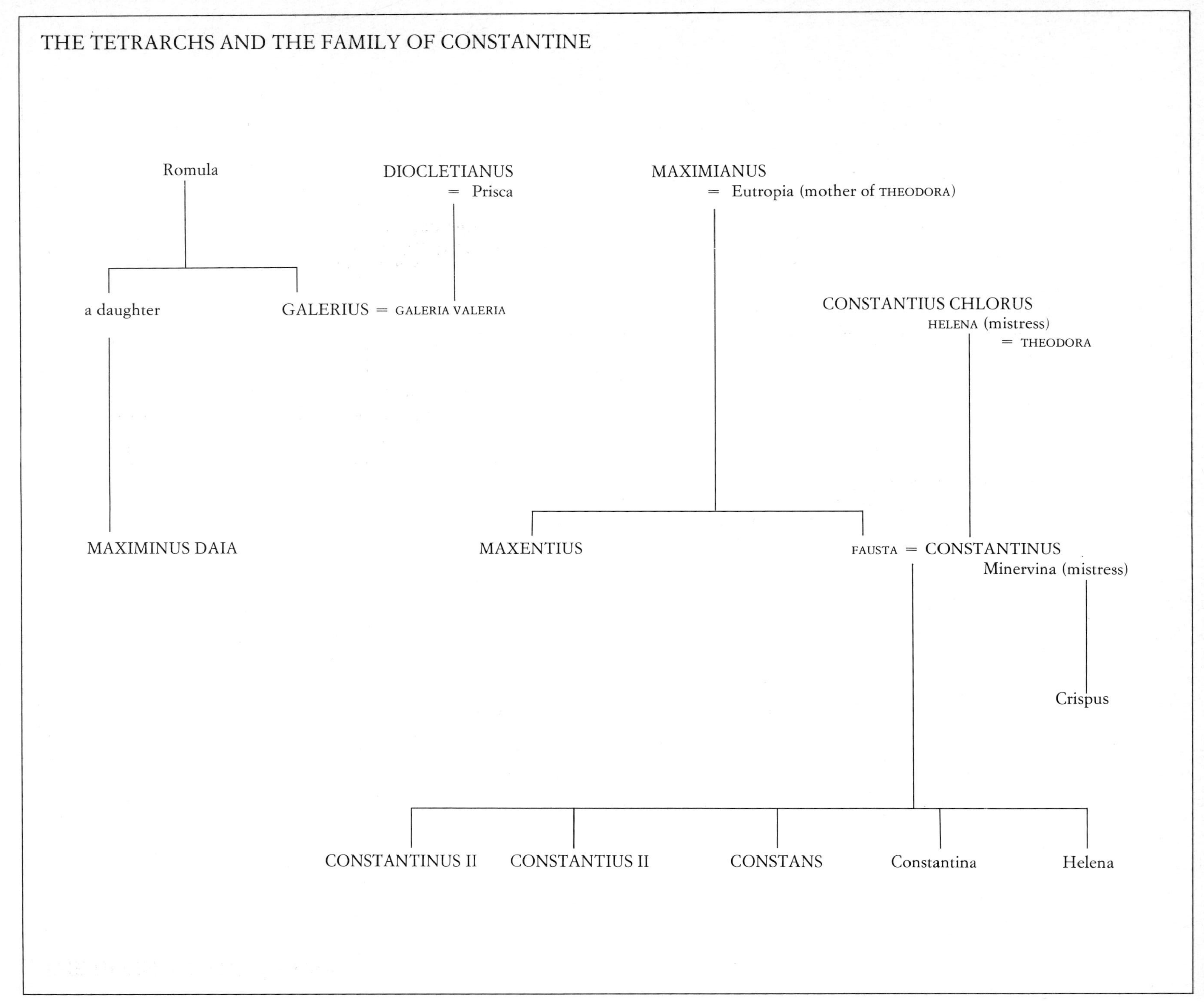
THE TETRARCHS AND THE FAMILY OF CONSTANTINE
Romula
DIOCLETIANUS
= Prisca
MAXIMIANUS
= Eutropia (mother of THEODORA)
a daughter
GALERIUS = GALERIA VALERIA
CONSTANTIUS CHLORUS
HELENA (mistress)
= THEODORA
MAXIMINUS DAIA
MAXENTIUS
FAUSTA = CONSTANTINUS
Minervina (mistress)
Crispus
CONSTANTINUS II
CONSTANTIUS II
CONSTANS
Constantina
Helena

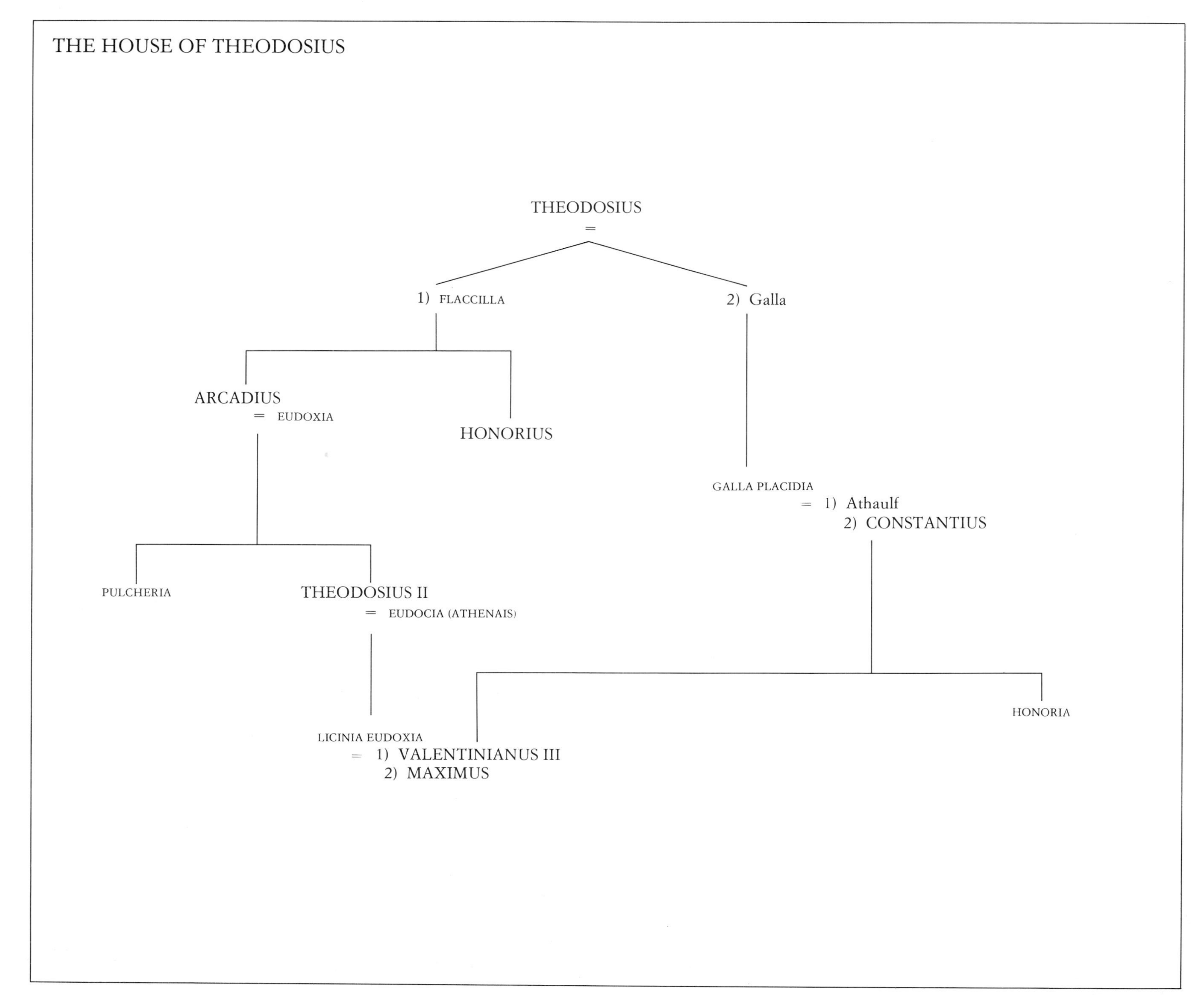
THE HOUSE OF THEODOSIUS
THEODOSIUS
=
1) FLACCILLA
2) Galla
ARCADIUS
= EUDOXIA
HONORIUS
GALLA PLACIDIA
= 1) Athaulf
2) CONSTANTIUS
PULCHERIA
THEODOSIUS II
= EUDOCIA (ATHENAIS)
HONORIA
LICINIA EUDOXIA
= 1) VALENTINIANUS III
2) MAXIMUS

# Introduction

In no society of the ancient world did women enjoy such consideration and esteem as in that of Rome, and nowhere in antiquity did they play such a role in the affairs of men. Unlike the Greek woman, segregated in the narrow world of the gynaeceia, mistress of her slaves but actually a slave herself, the Roman woman was never merely a toy or a wife whose sole purpose was to bear her husband sons. Even in the rustic and martial society of the first centuries of the Republic, she shared with her husband authority over their children and slaves, she was present with him at banquets, she carefully administered the domestic economy, she took part in his public life as companion and not infrequently as counsellor, and she directed the small textile industry which provided clothing for all the members of every patrician Roman household from the *pater familias* to the lowest slave. "Casta fuit, domum servavit, lanam fecit" (She was chaste, kept house, worked wool): these brief words of the funeral inscription of an unknown Roman matron sum up with archaic simplicity a life-role that from its beginning had nothing in common with the cloistered and unedifying atmosphere of the gynaeceia of classical Greece.

For this social life (which we might term completely modern) the Roman woman was prepared from earliest childhood. Boys and girls grew up and played freely together. They attended their first lessons together, where the future men and women of the Republic learned to read, to write, and to do simple arithmetic under the guidance of their tutor. During the last centuries of the Republic, because of greater refinement of manners and the diffusion of Greek culture, the girls of good family continued their education under the guidance of able instructors. They studied Latin and Greek literature, they learned to play the lyre, to sing, to dance, to carry on interesting conversations, in brief to become perfect companions of the cultivated men who already constituted such a large part of higher Roman society. This refinement of manners and intellectual development which the Greeks of the classical age sought and found only outside the walls of their houses in the company of select *hetairai* (courtesans) became part of the social equipment of every Roman woman of good family, at least in the last years of the Republic and during the entire high empire. But, as compared to the great Athenian *hetairai,* the Roman woman was also (as we have noted) an able domestic administrator, director and coordinator of the work of the slaves who made up her household. Once married, which occurred at a young age, the Roman girl became a matron with total liberty of movement similar to that of the women of today. She left her house, she went to the baths, she went to the market, she exchanged visits with her friends, she accompanied her husband when invited out, and returned with him in the wee hours, she went to the theatre, and she undertook journeys.

During the last century of the Republic, the Roman patrician lady had completed the last and most important step on the road towards moral and social equality by obtaining legal independence. Though previously, from an economic point of view, she had been the eternal ward of her father, her husband or her guardian, marriage *sine manu* [1], almost universally adopted by patrician or well-to-do families by the end of the Republican period, permitted her to

1. Unlike the traditional marriage *cum manu,* in which the bride became part of her husband's family, in marriage *sine manu* the wife continued to belong to her own family with its rights of inheritance.

keep and administer all the goods she had or could acquire with her own means. This important right was quickly extended (by the indirect means of legal fictions) to the unmarried woman as well, who, according to traditional law, would have been subject to her father or guardian for life.

It was not even unknown for Roman women to participate in mass demonstrations (as one calls them today). On more than one occasion they massed in the Forum or in other public places to obtain laws or provisions which interested them from the magistrates. One may recall, for example, Livy's account of the famous demonstration of 195 B.C. in which the more prominent Roman matrons demonstrated for the abolition of the sumptuary legislation of the Lex Oppia[2].

2. *Ab urbe condita,* 34, 1 ff.

The social and legal position of the Roman matron, as well as the liberty she enjoyed, were nonetheless undermined by a custom which is difficult if not impossible for us to understand. The marriage of a patrician woman (or at least her first marriage) was never her free choice. Her engagement was made by her parents while she was still a child, and the Roman woman of high station passed, an unconscious pledge of alliance among the families of the ruling class, from her childhood games to the home of a husband usually as young as herself. Thus at 13, 14 or 15 years of age, the Roman woman found herself married to a man selected not by the dictates of her heart but by the political advantage of her family. As long as the moral fiber of Republican Rome retained its hold on men's souls, as long as character, fidelity, simplicity, dedication to husband and children were inculcated not by segregation but through education, religion, and the force of public sentiment, women in general accepted the fate of these arranged marriages. But when, with the increase of personal riches toward the end of the Republic, Rome was transformed into a great metropolis in which men, customs and cults of every part of the world were mingled, and the convulsion of the Civil Wars brought the collapse of the old system and old ways of thought, belief in the traditional puritanism of the Roman aristocracy was destroyed and with it feminine morality.

Finally, there was divorce. In the marriage *sine manu* the wife, in the sight of the law, continued to belong to her paternal family. Since this kind of marriage did not constitute a formal contract, its only foundation was the continued cohabitation of the partners and their agreement to consider themselves man and wife. To dissolve the marriage one had only to separate. "Tuas res tibi habeto" (Take your goods) was the formula pronounced by the husband to his wife. Moreover, if he did not wish to make this declaration in person, he needed only to write it or send the communication through a slave. Nothing else was necessary.

In spite of this procedural simplicity, there had been a time when divorce was considered an act of great importance and gravity. But in the debacle of the Civil Wars in the last years of the Republic, the dictates of ever-changing interests and alliances among the families caused its spread among the patrician class in a disastrous fashion. In the age of Caesar there were many aristocratic women who had had three or four husbands, not because of their own frivolity but because they were influenced or forced into divorce and remarriage by their own husbands or by their fathers, who were carrying out their own political ambitions in this way. Early marriage and ease of divorce were therefore the two termites which undermined the morals of the family in the highest circles of Romans in the evening of the Republic and during the Empire. There were, of course, numerous outstanding exceptions, of which we shall have reason to speak.

This brief introduction to the moral, social and legal state of the woman of the Roman aristocracy is necessary to introduce the reader to the world of the women to whom this book is dedicated. These are the women who, as mothers, wives, daughters, sisters, and mistresses of emperors, found themselves now in the roles of faithful companions, now in the roles of bitter enemies, precipitated amid the fortunes of the absolute lords of a limitless empire which extended from the shadows of the forests of Britain to the deserts of Africa and which embraced in its immense domain cities facing the Atlantic and others perched on the bastions of the Caucasus.

The lives of some of these women are chronicled in the unforgettable pages of Tacitus. These are the ladies of the Julio-Claudian dynasty, Livia, Julia, Antonia, the two Agrippinas, Messalina, Octavia, Poppaea. They are tragic figures, sketched on the background of a bloody age, contrivers and victims at the same time of a fatal Shakespearean chain of dramatic events.

Weaker voices recount the lives of other imperial ladies, the wives and the daughters of the Flavians with whom the first century of the empire ends. But in the gossip and superficiality of Suetonius we can make out the tragic lives of Julia and Domitia.

Thus, in the new century which begins with the brilliant undertakings of Trajan, the majestic shadow of that new Livia, Plotina, and the profiles of Sabina and of the two Faustinas, mother and daughter, seem blurred and far away as if they were seen through a mist through which the fragmentary information of Dio Cassius and that mixture of truth and fiction which goes under the name of the *Historia Augusta* breaks through here and there like the rays of the sun, enabling us to guess at rather than to understand the personalities, the grandeur and the miseries of these imperial women. While the century of Trajan, Hadrian and Marcus Aurelius passes in the ignominiousness of an empire put up for sale by the Praetorian Guard, the third century begins with a dynasty of awe-inspiring, omnipotent women of the Severan house, the four Julias, natives of distant Emesa. The same century ends, in its turn, with the obscure wives of the ephemeral lords of war elevated and destroyed by the legions, at times in a single day.

In the fourth and fifth centuries there emerged by the side of their glorious or obscure husbands the disturbing and tragic figures of Valeria, Helena, Fausta and finally, when everything around is falling in ruin, those of Galla Placidia, Honoria, Pulcheria, Eudocia, beautiful and cultivated "Girl of Athens" born in that pagan city, to die a Christian in Jerusalem, a figure emblematic of a world dissolving to be born again under a new and different light.

Time has blurred the figures and erased the profiles of all these women who through five centuries accompanied their husbands in guiding the largest empire of antiquity.

What were, then, the faces, the physical traits, of the heroines of Tacitus and the wives, daughters, mothers and sisters of emperors in these successive centuries? Roman sculpture cannot reply to this question. Only a few busts give us, with any assurance, the features of certain empresses. Others have been identified as portraits of this or that imperial lady, above all on the basis of coin portraits, but by far the greatest part of the Roman marbles which bore the features of the women of the Caesars ended in the lime kilns of the Dark Ages, while bronze busts fed the hunger for metals of the same period.

Agrippina, Domitia, Plotina, Helena, and so many others would be figures without a face if there did not exist the coins which, as a royal gesture of the emperors towards the women of their own family, carry their images. Coins, indispensable instruments of the Roman economy but also, as we shall see, an universal and at the same time all-pervading method of propaganda in a world without modern means of communication, prove in this way once again to be indispensable and precious documents for the historian. From the bowels of the earth where misers in fear of thieves or men in fear of wars and invasions secreted them in remote times, pieces of gold, denarii, sestertii, asses, and antoniniani give us the living images of those women whose lives and character are narrated by ancient documents. They preserve the images of others whose every memory has been destroyed by time, women such as Manlia Scantilla, Didia Clara, Paulina, Mariniana, and so many others who gaze in silence from their coins, a face, a name and titles of grandeur of which we have no other memory.

In this book we wish to offer to those interested in history, art, and numismatics a "gallery" of portraits of women, some of high artistic quality, which appear on the coins of the Roman empire. We shall have occasion to treat the lives of some of these women fully; to others we shall give only a passing nod. And in the representation of the Roman empresses we shall follow the centuries-long artistic evolution of Roman portraiture which, beginning with the uncompromising verism of certain figures of the first century, conducts us through its slow but constant evolution to the massive and stylized figures of the art of the period of the Tetrarchs and thence to the cold idealization of the early Byzantine period.

The first chapter will be dedicated to the portraits of two women who were never Augustae. However, they had a decisive role in the bitter and bloody birth of the Empire and their names came to symbolize to the subjects of the nascent empire two opposite conceptions of life and of the world. These two women were Octavia and Cleopatra.

Chapter 1

# THE BIRTH OF THE EMPIRE

## Cleopatra and Octavia: the East against the West.

Octavian, Antony, Cleopatra, Octavia: there are few instances in history in which we encounter figures so antithetical, personalities so diverse as those of the four protagonists of the bloody birth of the Roman empire.

First of all, the two men. With the name of Caesar always on their lips, the aspirant heirs of his power and his glory, Octavian and Antony, divided the empire after the battle of Philippi and prepared themselves for the final duel for absolute supremacy. Compared with the figure of the dead dictator, they seem two incomplete beings, two half-Caesars, to each of which nature had given some but only some of the qualities that had made the assassinated dictator such an exceptional man. In brief, we might say that Octavian was Caesar without fascination or generosity and that Antony was Caesar without the superior political intelligence and acuteness of his great general.

To be sure, the young grand-nephew of the assassinated dictator had the quick intuition, the perfect sense of opportunism, and the clear political vision of his adoptive father. But these gifts, grand as they were, were chilled by a cold detachment. He was small in stature, had a large nose, his coloring was unhealthy, his teeth were irregular, and by turns he was forced to shield himself from the heat of summer by donning a wide-brimmed hat or the cold of winter by donning four tunics, one above the other. Octavian certainly did not have the *physique du rôle* of a leader of armies or a charismatic captain. With his uncaptivating appearance there went an ugly disposition of inexorable cruelty, faithlessness and calculation, untouched by a drop of that human sympathy or that noble generosity which were Caesar's winning gifts. It was not without reason that on the field of Philippi the republican officers when brought before the two victorious generals as prisoners immediately following the battle saluted Antony as "imperator" while keeping a chilly silence before Octavian.

Antony was the antithesis of his younger rival. He was a fine figure of a man with a bit of the gladiator and ruffian about him so popular with soldiers and common folk. From his old commander he had learned the art of arousing enthusiasm and even adoration in his own troops. A gifted orator, he used his instincts astutely on the death of Caesar, the one moment at which Caesar's opponents could have triumphed. He exercised a fascination which Octavian lacked, but he possessed neither the intelligence nor the iron determination of his rival. He could be generous without guile. On the eve of the battle of Actium, in a magnificent gesture, he sent the consul Domitius Ahenobarbus who had betrayed him and passed over to the camp of Octavian the enormous patrimony and following which that patrician had abandoned. But nonetheless this man whom Renan defines as "An enormous child capable of conquering a world but incapable of resisting a pleasure" was an impulsive and high-spirited nature who had neither the intelligence of Caesar nor his power of synthesis or quick intuition. In the same way as his physical nature was prone to every form of excess, the irresistible and immediate impulses of his heart determined many of the decisions of his life. It was one of these impulses which at the battle of Actium led him to abandon the decisive action to follow once again the woman who was his undoing.

Between these two men struggling for the empire two women, Octavia, great for the nobility of her soul, and Cleopatra, great for intelligence, courage and determination, became symbols and living examples of two opposite conceptions of life for the Romans of the time. Coming as they did from two different worlds, it is difficult to say today which of the two was more injurious to a man whom both called husband [1]. It is certain that Cleopatra, from their encounter at Tarsus to the last act of the tragedy played out in the waters of Actium, dragged Antony always deeper into the abyss in which she too was to perish. The decorous composure of Octavia, her dignified and submissive behavior in the face of a man who had abandoned and repudiated her without reason, her repeated refusal to be used by her brother Octavian against her faithless spouse, undoubtedly had the very effect on many important Romans that the cold-blooded Octavian desired and kept men's sympathy and resources from his rival in the triumvirate.

The portraits of these two women who linked their destiny to the struggle between the successors of Caesar in such a fatal fashion have been preserved for us on a number of coins. The queen of Egypt, the last of the house of Lagus, appears on a bronze coin (Plate I) which is perhaps the last coin of the dying Ptolemaic kingdom and thus of Egypt as a sovereign state. The head which appears on this coin is without question a portrait. The nose is slightly aquiline, large and decisive, the forehead prominent and intelligent. These features show that the artist, following a practice of many Hellenistic engravers, has attempted in no way to idealize his regal model but has sought to offer us a boldly realistic portrait. The woman shown on this coin is not beautiful, and Cleopatra is not beautiful in her few other portraits which have come down to us across the two millennia. The few other coins which preserve the image of the queen and her bust in the British Museum have the same slightly aquiline nose, the same broad nostrils, and the same angular line of the forehead [2]. Nor would the description of her given by historians make us think that the last queen of the Ptolemaic dynasty was a woman of exceptional physical gifts. "Her beauty", says Plutarch, "was not beyond compare, nor such as to strike one at first sight", and he adds that Octavia, who later became Antony's wife, was far more beautiful. But Plutarch also adds that Cleopatra's conversation had an irresistible fascination, and that her very expression, as well as her conversation and the style which emanated from her whole being, exercised an inescapable attraction [3].

Hardly a beauty, and of so small a stature that she could be smuggled into Caesar's presence wrapped in a rug carried on the shoulder of a slave, Cleopatra nonetheless had an exceptional and unsettling fascination, the proof of which is her becoming in succession the mistress of two all-powerful leaders engaged in the conquest of the world. Neither Caesar nor Antony was a man

1. Antony, in accord with the pact of Brundisium, married Octavia in October of 40 B.C. Three years later, in all probability, he married Cleopatra with the rites of the Egyptian religion.

2. There are no other true portraits of Cleopatra. The reliefs on the walls of the temple of Denderah and other Egyptian temples have completely conventionalized representations of the queen. The so-called "head of Cleopatra" in the museum at Alexandria probably does not represent the last queen of Egypt, as many archaeologists have believed.

3. Plutarch, *Parallel Lives,* Antony 27.

to avoid an amorous adventure. But to have bound them to her for years, in different ways to be sure, to have made them commit acts which brought on one harsh criticism and on the other complete ruin proves that the fascination of the queen and the sensual power of her personality were exceptional. Both men, although they had known her at different times of life and in very different conditions, were attached to her by love and hate from which they did not free themselves until their death. It is only in this way that one can explain the apparent contradiction in Caesar, who took her with him to Rome, where he had his family and where there was scandal and criticism emanating from the ruling class which had many reasons for hostility toward him. But after showing so clearly that he could not live without Cleopatra, he mentioned neither her nor their son in his will. The same thing happened to Antony. After being parted from her by the political marriage with Octavia, he was recalled to her by an irresistible impulse and only in the last days before Actium, when everyone begged Antony to leave the queen for the good of his cause, when every night Roman senators and allied chiefs, indignant and offended by the total subjection of the triumvir before the Egyptian, went over to Octavian's camp with men and information, between Antony and Cleopatra there fell a veil of bitterness and suspicion. To her bitterness with him corresponded his fear of being poisoned by her. Only in this final twilight of his fortune did Antony probably come to his senses and understand the damage that her presence in the camp wrought to his cause. But when, in the midst of the battle, he saw the white sails of the 60 Egyptian ships unfurled to the wind and understood that the queen had taken flight, that blind love with which Cleopatra had bound him to herself for so many years prevailed over everything else. "What was once said as a joke, that the soul of the infatuated lives in the body of the object of his affections, was here revealed as a profound truth, as if he were already part of her person and were constrained to move with her wherever she might go. As soon as he saw her ships departing, he abandoned those that fought and gave their lives for him to follow her" [4].

4. Plutarch, *Parallel Lives,* Antony 66.

Antithesis and opponent of Cleopatra, Octavia, the sister of Augustus, appears on coins of gold and silver struck to announce to the world the ephemeral reconciliation of the two rivals made in 40 B.C. after the pact of Brundisium. Octavia, the hostage of the alliance, more beautiful and perhaps younger than Cleopatra, married Mark Antony, and the mints of Greece and Asia Minor, the territories in the hands of the ex-lieutenant of Caesar, hastened to issue coins carrying the images of the newlyweds on their two faces. For the first time in the history of Rome, the portrait of a living woman, sister and wife respectively of the two autocrats of the Romans, appeared on coins for propagandistic and honorific motives, a thing which the outlook of Republican Rome would never have tolerated. In illustrating so many portraits of Augustae in the following chapters, we cannot forget this important fact: that from the final convulsions of the Republic there was born the new reality and above all the new outlook of the Empire.

If we can recognize in the coin portrait of Cleopatra only the outlines of a face and not the fascinating life which animated them, in the portrait of Octavia which appears on the fine coin illustrated in Plate II the artist has understood how to capture and imitate admirably the gentle and reserved fascination of this woman. Without making a portrait in the Greek style, that is without idealizing her and making her a cold goddess, but without dramatizing the image in the manner of many Hellenistic engravers by accentuating the salient features of the face, the unknown engraver of this beautiful aureus has understood how to create a living and breathing portrait in which the most profound spiritual characteristics of the person shine through a physical description in no way mechanical but nonetheless precise. In this small and delicate face an attentive observer can catch something that will remind him of certain coin portraits of Augustus recast in an image of beauty and femininity[5]. The nose is somewhat long, there is the same set of the mouth and the forehead, and in addition there is something indefinable which brings to mind the unmistakable face of the founder of the Empire. And yet, the thoughtful expression on the face, the slender, youthful neck, the dressing of the hair, at once simple and refined[6], the sense of fragility artfully created by setting the small female head in the large empty and uninscribed area of the coin, contribute to make this image a portrait vibrating with extraordinary inner spirituality.

On the other face of this magnificent piece (Plate III) the same able artistic hand has captured with equal psychological intuition the character, more than the physical features, of Mark Antony. In contrast to the small fragile head of Octavia which is almost lost in the empty field of the coin, we find the features of Antony menacingly accentuated and sensual, and in contrast to her troubled expression, his satisfied smile. To the silence of inscription around the simple portrait of the woman, there is opposed the resonant titulature which surrounds the head of the general, lord of half the empire: M ANTONIUS IMP III VIR R P C[7].

This, then, is the portrait of Octavia, the antithesis of Cleopatra, the woman who in obedience to her brother and for reasons of state, as was the custom of Roman noblewomen, married the man who until that moment had been the enemy of her family. Perhaps Octavia finally fell in love with the impulsive and spirited soldier whom the manipulations of high politics had placed at her side. Certainly the heart of this refined lady compared his volcanic spontaneity and his instinctive and exuberant nature to the cold untrustworthiness and unquenchable determination of her brother. And perhaps because of this silent consideration, this generous lady, who would have wished to be no more than a good wife, accepted abandonment and repudiation with muted dignity, without offering herself to the all-too-easy game of her brother. Though Antony, at the call of invisible powers, dashed towards his destiny, Octavia would never become an instrument of his enemies, so that after the tragic conclusion of the great duel she accepted into her own house and brought up beside the children whom Antony had given her the unfortunate children that the exuberant triumvir had had by his previous wife Fulvia, and by Cleopatra.

And so, with the battle of Actium and with the double suicide of Antony and Cleopatra a year after the battle, an epoch closes forever.

The two women who characterized this dramatic denouement have suffered

5. For example, the coin reproduced at the top of Plate VI.

6. In the last years of the Republic and under the Empire, fashion and personal taste show infinite variety in feminine hairdressing. Ovid, who liked to describe in minute particulars the hairstyle of Roman matrons, declares emphatically that it would be easier to count the leaves of an oak tree or the bees of Hybla than the different hairstyles invented every day (*Art of Love,* 3.130). However, in the time of Octavia, to judge by the testimony of coins and statues, the hairstyles still have a certain simplicity, even in their variety. The taste for braids was still very common. In our portrait of Octavia, we see a large braid that, leaving the forehead and dividing the hairdressing in two like a part, descends, becoming slenderer, towards the neck where, together with two other locks brought from the temples, it forms a knot of hair. Behind the ears two long curls descend on the neck, lightening the somewhat cold and geometric structure of the hairstyle with a touch of grace and vivacity.

7. MARCUS ANTONIUS IMPERATOR TRIUMVIR REI PUBLICAE CONSTITUENDAE (Mark Antony, Triumvir for the Reconstitution of the Republic).

different fates in the historical tradition. Octavia, the symbol of every womanly virtue, was justly considered a model of Roman simplicity and purity. Cleopatra, the Egyptian, as she was degradingly called, was represented by the writers and poets of the imperial period as the very personification of evil, the tragic Circe who had sacrificed thousands of Roman lives to her own ambition. But, as is well known, history is written by the victors, and today we can detect in the adventurous life of the last queen of Egypt something more and something different than the all-too-easy slander of a Plutarch, of a Dio Cassius, or of a Suetonius. True, she was a seductress, but let us not forget that we have no knowledge of other affairs in her life than her long relation with Caesar and with Antony. Moreover, she was certainly no more corrupt than many ladies of that Roman aristocracy which so tenaciously opposed her. And she employed her charm in an attempt to save her dying land, and in a grandiose and audacious plan to make it the center of the new empire which should rise from the ashes of the Republic. She was certainly cruel in killing her sister, brother, and anyone who blocked her way, but such crimes, in each case dictated by the pitiless logic of necessity, are small in respect to what all the preceding monarchs of the Ptolemaic dynasty, perhaps the most monstrous line of perverted beasts that have ever existed, did out of pure sadism. Cleopatra was also a cultivated, intelligent woman, endowed with that precise determination which Antony had always lacked. Finally, she knew how to die the death of a true queen, escaping ignominy in the triumph of Augustus.
Among the prisoners who followed the triumphal chariot of the victor in chains there was not the proud queen of Egypt, only her portrait: "Curled around her arm there was shown the asp with which she killed herself" [8].

8. Plutarch, *Parallel Lives,* Antony 86. It was not by chance that Cleopatra chose to die by the bite of the asp. This means, which to us seems particularly repugnant, was chosen because in ancient Egyptian religious beliefs death by the bite of serpents, snakes or crocodiles opened the way to apotheosis.

Chapter 2

# THE JULIO-CLAUDIANS

## In the House of Augustus: Livia, Antonia, Julia.

In spite of chronic colds, gallstones, and a weak liver, the victor of Actium, now alone at the summit of power, had a long life. His friends and associates of former times one by one passed on. Victims of diseases or of the irresistible course of years, the strong men who had been his companions in the tumultuous years of the Civil War disappeared one after the other, while the aged emperor in his modest house on the Palatine, surrounded now by a respect which bordered on religious veneration, seemed, among the ruin of so many vigorous natures, to be alone in holding off the assault of time. For the rising tide of new generations, Philippi and Actium were already distant events, evermore rigidified into history, almost mythical material now for the glorifying recitals of poets.

When at last on a hot day of August, A.D. 14, the seventy-seven-year-old emperor understood that for him too there had come the moment to close his eyes forever, his last thought and last words were for Livia, the faithful wife who for so many years had shared his destiny: "Livia nostri coniugii memor vive ac vale" (Livia, live in memory of our years together, and farewell)[1].

1. Suetonius, *Lives of the Twelve Caesars,* 2.99.

Fifty-two years earlier, in 38 B.C., Octavian (Plate VI above), the youngest of the Triumviri Reipublicae Constituendae, the colleague of Antony and of Lepidus in the military dictatorship established after the death of Caesar, urgently sought the opinion of the College of Pontifices, that is to say the highest religious authority of the Republic, on the question of whether a pregnant woman could be divorced and remarry before giving birth. The reply of the pontiffs was as follows: she could not do so if her pregnancy was still in doubt, but if it was certain there was no obstacle. A few days after receiving this communication, the twenty-five-year-old triumvir divorced Scribonia and married the nineteen-year-old Livia Drusilla, already mother of a boy and now again pregnant. The marriage on her part was made possible by a similarly rapid divorce from her husband Tiberius Claudius Nero. This strange individual had not only handed over his wife without a sigh but even gave her a dowry as if he were her father, and participated merrily in the wedding dinner. Three months later, Livia bore a child who was called Drusus Claudius Nero and whom Octavian had quickly given over to Livia's former husband as a thing not belonging to himself[2].

2. There has naturally been a long discussion over the paternity of the child given the name Drusus. Suetonius relates that the following joke circulated widely: "Lucky people manage to have children in three months" (*Lives of the Twelve Caesars,* 5.1).

Although Roman morals had become extremely elastic, this event could hardly fail to arouse scandal. Was it possible that Octavian, so cold and so calculating, had lost his head over a woman at this point? And Livia, the sage and moderate Livia, who for half a century at court was to play the slightly frigid role of the perfect matron of irreproachable morals, Livia, who with her own hands made her husband's garments, the example of domestic virtues cited by Augustus before the entire senate, and also, we should not forget, the intelligent and cautious counsellor of her husband in the most delicate affairs, was this a woman capable of permitting herself to be overthrown by such a lecherous love affair and suffer such an obvious infatuation? For us today, after two millennia, it is certainly difficult to know the facts. But a knowledge of the character of the two protagonists and the consequences of their scandalous marriage leads us towards a probable explanation: that this was a political marriage, so common in that time among the members of the Roman aristocracy.

Who was Livia? She was a woman generously endowed with beauty, intelligence, and influential relatives. She was a member, in fact, of the main house of the Claudii, a family which was among the most powerful of the still-powerful Roman aristocracy. Her father, Marcus Livius Drusus Claudianus, proscribed by the triumvirs in 43, committed suicide after Philippi. Her husband also belonged to the Claudii and had fought first for Caesar against Pompey and then, during the Perusine war, for Lucius Antonius and the Republic against Octavian himself. By means of the marriage now celebrated, Octavian, the youngest of the triumvirs, the adopted son of the great Caesar but in reality the simple grandson of a rich usurer of Velitrae, joined the highest Roman nobility, acquiring prestige, valuable friends, and alliances. The Claudii, for their part, bound themselves to the revolution which the old Roman senatorial aristocracy, of which they were among the highest members, already realized they could not overcome but realized, all the same, how to tame.

The impresario of this spectacular maneuver which united a member of the high Republican aristocracy with the new warlord was perhaps actually Livia's first husband, and if it was he, his hopes were certainly not deluded. In the house of the man who had proscribed her father, Livia was for more than fifty years the intelligent and discreet guardian genius of the old Rome. And in the end it was Tiberius, the son of Livia and Tiberius Claudius Nero, who inherited the principate which had been created to strangle the power of the senatorial aristocracy.

However, in the mysterious way of destiny, Augustus and Livia loved each other for all their life, and none of the family tragedies which struck the house of Augustus could cast a shadow on their union.

The portrait of this strong and level-headed woman who had such influence on the founder of the empire is preserved on bronze coins. In his cautious policy of diminishing the prerogatives and powers of the aristocracy, without injuring their pride through useless display of power, Augustus never wished Livia's image to appear on coins. He well knew that such an act would have provoked criticism in the more conservative circles of the patricians. To be sure, there was a precedent. But the coins with the portraits of Mark Antony and of Augustus's sister Octavia, we should not forget, had been minted purposefully to commemorate and advertise the matrimonial alliance that could have brought the peace all desired. Moreover, they had been struck by greek and oriental mints, not at Rome. Now, however, Augustus was the princeps, and to reproduce the portrait of his wife on a Roman coin would have been an unnecessary insult to the senatorial aristocracy for whom such an act would have seemed another gesture of Caesarism. It was thus left to Tiberius, coming to the throne after the death of Augustus, to give this honor to his mother in A.D. 22 or 23, on the occasion of the great honors decreed by the senate to the octogenarian empress. But even then he introduced the portrait of his mother on coins in an indirect way, by giving three divinities, Pietas, Iustitia and Salus Augusta the features of the young Livia.

These coin portraits of the wife of Augustus reflect two tendencies which were to continue to exist together in Roman plastic art: the Greek idealized portrait and the realistic portrait of pure Italic origin. The classic lines of the lovely face which we can still admire on the dupondius illustrated in Plate V present no physical characteristic which might suggest a portrait. It is a striking face of a young woman with a Greek nose and a pure and noble expression. Beneath this diademed and fine head there is the legend IUSTITIA, and the unknown artist of the coin, in fact, has transfigured the face of a mortal woman in the perfect and severe image of the divinity. The dupondius shown in Plate IV is very different. In the face of Salus Augusta the engraver has actually shown the features of the wife of Augustus. The face has the same features as the marble head of Livia in the Copenhagen Museum: a marked jaw, lips pursed in a set expression, large eyes, and a strong-willed and slightly aquiline nose. Livia's hairstyle is simple. Her hair, parted at the crown of the head, falls in short waves toward the nape of the neck where it is gathered in a small chignon. Two long locks fall in ringlets on the neck behind her ears. It is a portrait which speaks to us. The expression of the face shows how much the artist has known how to penetrate into the deepest spirit of his subject, giving us not only a physically faithful representation but one that is also psychologically penetrating. How different is this portrait from the face of Octavia! The slightly cold beauty of Livia has nothing of the disarming sweetness of the sister of Augustus. It is a portrait of a rather different temper! The sharp intelligence, the strong and steady determination of the empress, are given by this portrait in a classical and powerful synthesis.

Another woman of whom Augustus could be proud is shown on coins. She is Antonia, the younger daughter of Mark Antony and Octavia[3].

A woman of famous beauty, she was married by Augustus to Drusus, the second son of Livia and Tiberius Claudius Nero[4]. Drusus, like his elder brother Tiberius, had been left by Livia with her former husband but later had come back to live with his mother when Tiberius Claudius Nero died leaving Augustus as his guardian. Antonia had three children by him: Germanicus, Livilla and Claudius, a man without ambition who was later to become emperor. When, in 9 A.D., Drusus died, without seeing his thirtieth year, the beautiful and noble Antonia refused to remarry and continued to live with Livia.

Wise, virtuous, intelligent and level-headed, this woman embodied in the emperor's eyes another example of the type of matron he would have wished to see become common in high Roman society. And in the disaster which death and corruption sowed in his family, Livia and Antonia remained to the end two irreplaceable sources of comfort for the old Augustus.

For Antonia to live with Livia, who was so different from her, was not difficult.

3. The younger Antonia was born in 37 B.C.

4. The elder of the two sons of Livia's first marriage was Tiberius, the future emperor. Drusus, as noted above, was born in 38, three months after the marriage of Livia and Augustus.

And when the aged empress died in A.D. 29, it was Antonia who continued to keep watch, reserved and modest, over her taciturn son Tiberius and to take guard against the machinations against the misanthrope of Capri which like serpents wound and unwound themselves continually in the Capitol. It was to be a messenger sent by Antonia (already approaching her seventieth year) in the night who warned the old emperor that the plot of Sejanus was about to break out at Rome[5]. Such solidarity and reciprocal esteem had never wavered during the preceding years, not even in the face of the grave suspicions which public opinion nurtured about the death of her son Germanicus, who with his youthful self-confidence represented for many Romans the opposite of the aged and taciturn Tiberius. The affection of the two old friends could not even be changed in the face of a double family tragedy when, during the repression of the conspiracy of Sejanus, Antonia's daughter Livilla was accused of having killed her own husband Drusus, the only son of Tiberius, with Sejanus's help and, fleeing to her mother, preferred suicide to facing investigation.

5. Sejanus, the praetorian prefect of Augustus, had conducted a bitter repression against the enemies of Tiberius and particularly the members of the party of Agrippina. Attaining the highest power, Sejanus in his turn organized a conspiracy against Tiberius which, however, was energetically repressed by the old emperor. Sejanus was executed with many of his followers in A.D. 31.

Of this great and unfortunate woman we have a youthful portrait which Claudius, her surviving son who became emperor in 41, dedicated to his mother who had died a few years earlier during the brief reign of Caligula[6]. Out of filial respect, her son has had Antonia portrayed on this beautiful dupondius (Plate VII) as she was in her youth, before the years and family tragedies had marked her face. It is a face with unmistakable traits, the nose a bit large but well-formed, the deep eyes, the slightly projecting upper lip, the soft mass of the hair bound in a simple way at the nape of the neck; a face of great beauty, with features quiet and strong at the same time, as one would expect of the character of this daughter of Mark Antony and Octavia. Encircling this strongly realistic portrait, one of the most beautiful images, and not only coin images, of Roman portraiture which we possess, there runs the legend ANTONIA AUGUSTA. The legend, in its lapidary simplicity and brevity, is important because it presents us with the title Augusta which a few years earlier Caligula, in an early demonstration of affection towards the women of his family, solemnly conferred on his old grandmother, on whom he had also bestowed all the privileges of the Vestal Virgins.

6. In A.D. 39, at seventy-six years of age.

In the house of Augustus there were not only Livia and Antonia. Julia, born in 39 B.C., daughter of Scribonia, was the only daughter of the emperor. It was in vain that Livia and Octavian hoped for a son. On the only occasion on which Livia conceived, the child was born prematurely and died. The entire affection of the princeps was thus reserved for this only daughter, and under the guidance of the cheerless and old-fashioned father that Augustus was and of Livia, the girl was brought up according to the old severe custom of the aristocracy, though to no purpose.

When, in 18 B.C., Augustus published his drastic laws for regulation of morals, certainly with the support of Livia and of the more traditional elements of the nobility, Julia was twenty-one years of age and was a member of the new generation that had not lived through civil wars and had entered into life eager for luxury, amusement, liberty, and all those novelties which undermined the state. Women began to rebel against arranged marriages. Remaining single and voluntary birth control led to the sterility of many illustrious families.

Tasteless luxury was ever more common and many young men of the aristocracy turned their backs on the army and the magistracies. It was necessary to correct this state of affairs and the emperor did so with three draconian laws: the Lex de Maritandis Ordinibus, with which he encouraged marriages with offspring by regulations designed to strike on the moral and financial level against the unmarried and against married persons who did not have children; the Lex Sumptuaria, by which excessive luxury in all its forms was prohibited; and the Lex de Adulteriis Coercendis, which constituted an effective martial law against adulteresses and their accomplices, on whom was inflicted the terrible penalty of exile for life and partial confiscation of their estates. The accusation of adultery had to be made by the husband or, if he could not or would not do so, by the father of the woman involved or by some other male citizen.

As these drastic laws were being promulgated, the twenty-one-year-old Julia had already caused comment about herself. Married young to Marcellus, the nephew of Augustus, son of Octavia's first marriage, she was early left a widow but not without having stirred up the ambition of her young husband and having caused much discontent as a result in the circle of the closest associates of her father. In 21 B.C., perhaps specifically to put an end to this notoriety and to satisfy her ambition, Augustus married her to Agrippa, his right arm and the second man of the Empire. At the side of a husband twenty-four years her senior, Julia quickly became just the opposite of Livia and everything that the wife of the princeps represented. Around the elegant young matron there gathered all the flamboyant society of Rome, brilliant young men and that wide fringe of self-destroying aristocracy that had already abdicated its historical duty. Julia was also a favorite of the people because they liked her silk gowns, her gaiety, her youthful abandon, her wild extravagance, and her measureless luxury. For the daughter of the emperor, the Lex Sumptuaria was a dead letter, and a dead letter as well was the law which prohibited wives from accompanying governors of provinces. In 16 B.C., Julia was in the East with Agrippa, always scintillating, always at the side of her martial husband at every banquet and at every official reception. The adulation of the Greeks and the Asiatics flattered and excited her. At Mytilene, she was called "the new Aphrodite", at Ephesus "Aphrodite Genetrix", at Paphos statues were erected to "the divine Julia". A Roman magistrate[7] in charge of coinage went so far as to place her image on coins in the guise of Diana. There began to appear in her company a brilliant young man, Sempronius Gracchus, a descendant of the celebrated tribunes. In 12 B.C., Agrippa died, leaving two daughters, Julia and Agrippina, and three sons, Gaius, Lucius and Agrippa (who was born after his father's death). Augustus displayed great affection toward these grandchildren of his own blood, in particular toward the three eldest, Gaius, Lucius and Julia.

The hope of settling once and for all the quarrel between his wife and his daughter drove Augustus to marry the restless widow to Livia's son. Thus Tiberius, the rigid and haughty aristocrat, profoundly in love with his own wife, was forced by his Machiavellian stepfather to divorce her and to marry Julia. But Tiberius had vision or intuition sharper than Agrippa's, and when

7. C. Marius Tromentina.

Julia's old lover Sempronius Gracchus reappeared on the scene, not being in a position to repudiate or denounce the daughter of the emperor, he decided to separate from her. Gaius and Lucius[8] had been adopted by Augustus some time before. But when plans were put afoot in Julia's circle for Gaius, who was only sixteen years old, to be elected consul, Tiberius opposed the project and in the face of the surrender of Augustus to the demands of his daughter, Tiberius abandoned public life and retired in voluntary exile to Rhodes.

8. Born, respectively, in 20 and 17 B.C.

From this moment on, behind the dispute which broke out between Tiberius and Julia, we see ever more clearly the shadow of Livia. And in this way, the tragedy of Augustus came to maturity. In 2 B.C. indisputable proof of Julia's adultery was brought to the emperor. Because her husband could not do so, it was Augustus, as prescribed in the Lex de Adulteriis, who was constrained to bring accusation against his daughter. Thus, at thirty-seven years of age, the woman who had been for so many years the center of attraction of the brilliant society of Rome was exiled forever, first to the tiny island of Pandateria and then to Rhegium in Calabria[9].

9. Julia was to die in exile in A.D. 14, after her father's death and the accession of Tiberius to the principate.

From that moment on, an implacable nemesis struck inexorably at the descendants of the killer of Caesarion[10]. On the 20th of August, A.D. 2, Lucius died at Marseilles, struck down by a rapid illness, and only twenty months later Gaius too died of injuries in Lycia. In A.D. 7 it was the turn of Agrippa who, already unbalanced, had to be confined on a remote island[11], and finally, in A.D. 8, the laws formulated by Augustus to contain the corruption of Roman morals turned once again against his afflicted descendants. Julia, his granddaughter, as beloved as Gaius and Lucius, was exiled to a desert island, like her mother ten years before. The inexorable Lex de Adulteriis dragged down with her lovers and accomplices, among whom was Ovid, the depraved poet of stylish Rome.

10. The son of Caesar and Cleopatra, who, still a boy, was assassinated on orders of Octavian after the double suicide of Antony and Cleopatra.

11. Planasia, where he was to die in A.D. 14.

There is a portrait of the daughter of Augustus, the frivolous and lightminded Julia, on a coin on which she is represented in the guise of Diana. The same face is also found on a *tessera*[12] which we reproduce in Plate VI below. But the portrait, which shows a hard face, sharp and distant, deceives us on this occasion. Perhaps Julia was never a beautiful woman, or perhaps her charm was like that of Cleopatra, made up of the brilliance of her glance, the melodiousness of her voice, that no sculptor, no engraver and no painter could represent.

12. Roman *tesserae* were copper tokens which served as entrance tickets for the circus and theatre. On one side they have a large numeral, evidently the section designated for the holder. The other side has the image of Augustus or another member of the imperial family or, in certain cases, even obscene designs.

## Between Tiberius and Caligula: the Awe-Inspiring Agrippina and her Daughters.

When, following the death of his two adopted grandsons, the aged Augustus decided to adopt Tiberius and associate him in the government of the Empire, he made two conditions. The first was that Tiberius adopt Germanicus, the elder son of his brother Drusus and Antonia. And second, perhaps in an attempt to quiet the continual friction between the Julians and the Claudians, the old emperor wished that the young and intelligent Germanicus marry his granddaughter, Agrippina, one of the daughters of Julia who had given him so much bitterness and sorrow.

Thus, when the victor of Actium closed his eyes forever, the seeds of new discord destined to trouble the imperial house were already sown. Tiberius, already past the prime of life[13], was a man of closed and introverted character and a rigid outlook. He was known to be a rather stingy administrator, and was the object of humor for his fondness for the grape (Biberius was a nickname that circulated among the people). This man certainly did not have the gift of awakening sympathy in others. After his miserable experience with Julia, he had decided not to marry and continued to live a bachelor life. His intimates were two older women, his mother Livia and his sister-in-law Antonia.

To this sad and solitary figure there was, contrasted and made even more attractive by the contrast, the personality of the young man whom the inflexible will of Augustus had destined to play the popular role of hereditary prince. Germanicus was endowed with everything that his adoptive father lacked. First of all, he was young, and with his youth he had charm, energy and courage. On a campaign in Germany, paying no heed to the warnings of the emperor, he had crossed the Rhine and decisively attacked the strongest barbarian tribes. This a few years after three whole legions had been swallowed up in the forests of Germany. But everyone likes audacity when crowned by luck, and Rome went wild for the young hero who, penetrating the unknown wilds beyond the Rhine, avenged the disaster of the Teutoburg forest.

Both to Germanicus's popularity and to his ever-increasing distance from the emperor there contributed not a little the wife whom Augustus had bestowed upon him. Agrippina was the perfect wife. She loved her husband, she embraced her work and motherhood with the seriousness of old Roman tradition. She had inherited neither the gay fashionableness, the taste for extravagance in clothes nor the careless morals of her frivolous and unfortunate mother. But one deadly thing they did have in common: love of intrigue and boundless ambition.

Having fed unceasingly the vanity of her popular husband, on his death at only thirty-four years of age in A.D. 19, probably from natural causes[14], Agrippina refused to resign herself but desperately gave credence to and even took a hand in spreading the rumor that attributed the premature death of the young hero to the envy of the unpopular imperial recluse.

From that moment on, there was no truce between Germanicus's widow and Tiberius. In a wild and delirious sequence of public scenes and intrigues, Agrippina became before all Rome the implacable accuser of the emperor[15]. The high opinion of Tiberius held by Antonia, the aged mother of Germanicus, was of no avail. Neither were all the efforts of the emperor to bring her to reason. Her consuming ambition, so bitterly frustrated by the tragic death of Germanicus, found a new outlet in their children, Nero and Drusus, who were entering adolescence. Like a mounting tide there gathered around her all those who for some reason hated Tiberius and found a respectable banner under which they could mask their private hatred of the princeps.

13. In A.D. 14, when he ascended the throne, he was 56.

14. The death of a young person was hardly strange in a period in which medicine was still in its infancy. A touch of pneumonia, a coughing fit, or indigestion was enough to cause death. A few years before, the two grandsons of Augustus, Gaius and Lucius, had died in the flower of youth, and a few years afterwards Drusus, the only son of Tiberius, was to die at thirty-eight, also, in all probability, from natural causes.

15. Agrippina's behavior when she refused to touch food or drink at a banquet given by Tiberius caused scandal in the entire city.

Bitter, disgusted and tired, the man who as a youth had mused through the pages of Horace and Livy on the restoration of the state through the aristocracy and harmony between all classes of the state retired more and more and for longer periods to the distant quiet of Capri. The triumph of his enemy was illusory, because he left behind to guard the state Sejanus, praetorian prefect, and an enemy far crueller and more prompt to action than the presumed poisoner of Germanicus.

As the storm grew near, Agrippina and her sons were slowly abandoned. True friends who dared remain at her side were removed one after the other through those terrifying judiciary machinations of which the history of every era offers such dreadful examples. When Livia died, at eighty-six years of age, in A.D. 29, the last invisible shield which protected Agrippina and her sons fell. A few months thereafter, the widow of Germanicus and her son Nero were brought to trial and condemned to exile. Nero committed suicide almost immediately. Agrippina, confined at Pandateria and Drusus, imprisoned at Rome, died, probably from suicide, a few years later.

When, in A.D. 37, the misanthrope of Capri closed his eyes forever, the empire passed by his will to a young man twenty-five years old, Gaius, nicknamed Caligula, the only living son of Agrippina and Germanicus, although it was too late for Julia's daughter to see her inexhaustible ambition satisfied.

One of the first official acts of the new emperor was to inter solemnly in the mausoleum of Augustus the remains of his mother and brother. In memory of Agrippina the young princeps had minted the splendid sestertius which we illustrate in Plates VIII and IX.

On the obverse of this coin a great engraver has handed down to us the dignified and severe profile of the enemy of Tiberius. It has the regular features of a sad patrician beauty still in style today. In the sharp features and the thin lips and the depth of the gaze we can almost read the salient contradictory traits of character of Julia's daughter, unrealized ambition, iron will, and moral strength. The hairstyle of the Claudian period, refined and complicated, foreshadows, though without excess, the incredible constructions of the Flavian epoch in the following century. But in spite of its artificiality and sophistication, it seems to suit the noble features of Agrippina. The locks, divided by a central part, fall widely and softly toward the nape of the neck where they are gathered and fall further on the neck in a large knot. Over the temples the locks are broken up into a soft mass of curls, while a long curl falls behind the ear over the neck, reaching down to the robe. Between the close folds of the robe and the wide rhythm of the *mélonfrisure,* barely interrupted by the play of curls on the temples, there is no clear break, but in a happily contrived counterpoint the artist has framed the severe aristocratic face of Agrippina with the rhythmically contrived waves of her locks and the folds of her robe. The legend surrounding the image, AGRIPPINA M F MAT C CAESARIS AUGUSTI[16], seems to sum up in a few words the dream, unrealized during her life, that was held by the widow of Germanicus.

16. AGRIPPINA MARCI FILIA MATER CAII CAESARIS AUGUSTI (Agrippina, daughter of Marcus, mother of Gaius Caesar Augustus).

On the reverse (Plate IX) there is a *carpentum,* the capacious vehicle reserved for the use of the ladies of the imperial family in the city, and its legend, SPQR

17. SENATUS POPULUSQUE ROMANUS MEMORIAE AGRIPPINAE (The Senate and the Roman People to the memory of Agrippina).

18. The inscription and the representation make allusion to the solemn procession in which the portrait of the dead princess mounted on a *carpentum* was drawn through the streets of Rome and through the Circus where there followed magnificent games in honor of Agrippina.

MEMORIAE AGRIPPINAE[17], reminded Caligula's subjects that the exile of Pandateria was returning to Rome in death but as the mother of an emperor[18].

The posthumous honors which the twenty-seven-year-old princeps gave his mother were not destined to remain an isolated case of filial piety. In addition to Gaius, Agrippina had left three daughters, Agrippina, Drusilla, and Julia Livilla, who, in A.D. 37, when their brother ascended the throne, were respectively 27, 20 and 19 years old. Caligula loved these girls, who had been catapulted from the terrors of persecution to imperial dignity, with that unbalanced but tender love which binds members of families crossed by destiny. The eternal desire for compensation of the poor man become rich, of the persecuted who suddenly finds himself at the height of power, was expressed not only through the posthumous exaltation of his mother and the title Augusta given as a filial tribute to his grandmother Antonia but also in the honors that Gaius heaped on his three sisters. They received all privileges reserved for the Vestal Virgins. The emperor had them seated at the games in seats as important as his own. And he ordered that in the augural prayers for the protection of his rule there be included a prayer for their happiness. Honors such as these given to young women were still unheard-of at this time and profoundly foreign to Roman custom and outlook. As never before, the aristocracy felt itself mortally endangered by this young iconoclast who, out of devotion to his own family, broke ancient tradition that had been respected for centuries.

Subsequently the wave of family affection was extended to include the memory of his great-grandfather Mark Antony while his orientalizing and graecophile policies became a pathological mania[19]. In the manner of a pharaoh or a Ptolemy (and the name of Cleopatra reverberated menacingly in every mind), the mad emperor had decided to marry his sister Drusilla and in preparation made a will in which he disposed of his possessions and, among these, of the empire as if it were his personal property. He was not able to carry out his plan because Drusilla died in A.D. 38 and Caligula, further unbalanced by his grief, made her a goddess, imposed her worship on all the cities of the empire, erected a temple to her, and created a body of twenty priests to carry out her cult, decreeing, moreover, that her birthday be a solemn feast. At last his morbid and deranged affection turned to hatred when his remaining sisters sought to intervene with him or to counsel him. In A.D. 38 Julia and in A.D. 39 Agrippina were forced again to take that road of exile to which tragedy had accustomed their family. The aged Antonia died in silence, she too having broken completely with her mad grandson. Caligula's paranoiac frenzy made and broke three marriages in three years. Livia Orestilla, Lollia Paulina, and Milonia Caesonia, mere shadows of whom we know only the names, appear briefly on the stage of empire to disappear without leaving the faintest trace.

19. As soon as he was made emperor, Caligula introduced Isis to the Roman pantheon and prohibited the annual commemoration of the battle of Actium.

On the 24th of January A.D. 41, at last, Cassius Chaerea, an officer of the Praetorian Guard, brought an end to Gaius's delirium. The last son of Agrippina thus died by assassination at only twenty-nine years of age[20].

20. His last wife, Caesonia, and their child were killed with him.

Time has erased the features of Drusilla, his favorite, and of his other sister Julia, who was also destined to die young. Of Agrippina, who was at this time bringing up in the ancient and severe Roman tradition a little boy with red hair by the name of Nero, we shall speak later. There is, however, a representation honoring the three young women on a sestertius which Gaius had coined on his accession to power (Plate X).

This coin is a pathetic testimony to the unbalanced explosion of family affection on the part of the young and newly-crowned emperor. On its reverse it shows us the three sisters of Caligula as divinities, Agrippina, the eldest, leaning on a column and symbolizing Securitas, Julia, the youngest, holding a rudder in her right hand and representing Fortuna[21]. In the center Caligula's favorite, Drusilla, holds a patera, symbol of Concordia, in her lowered right hand. The entire majestic and harmonious composition has a tasteful architectural quality. The figures of the three women divide the wide spaces of the large bronze coin like columns. The repetition of folds in their dress, the common pose marked by the bending of the right leg, the repeated curve of the cornucopias, all reinforce rather than break up the rhythm of the composition. And the clear sequence of the letters of the names of the sisters of Gaius also seem to be pilasters and architraves of some imaginary gateway. Solid and massive, like the terrain on which one erects buildings, the two letters in the exergue[22] seem to support on their heavy arching forms the entire weight of the architectural composition above them. None of the coins illustrated in this book is so typical of Roman art which shared the deeply practical and concrete nature of the people that developed it and found its best expression precisely in the field of monumental architecture.

21. Only traces of the rudder are visible in the coin illustrated here.

22. SC, abbreviation of Senatus Consulto (by decree of the Senate).

## The Women of Claudius and Nero: Messalina, Agrippina, Poppaea.

In the confusion that followed the assassination of Caligula, the soldiers discovered the fifty-year-old Claudius, the last surviving son of Drusus and Antonia, terrorized and hidden behind a curtain[23]. Son of a popular hero, and brother of Germanicus, whose memory was literally venerated by the soldiers, the trembling emperor-elect was brought to the praetorian camp and while the senate lost itself in pointless discussions of the restoration of the liberties of the republic, Claudius was raised to the principate by the troops.

Who was Claudius? His mother Antonia called him a caricature of a man, and to berate someone's stupidity she was wont to say pitilessly, "More of a fool than my son Claudius". His great-uncle Augustus talks about him in letters to Livia mentioned by Suetonius[24] as a pitiable child, to be sure, but also as a grave embarrassment for the imperial family. It is a fact that the last son of the great Drusus and Antonia was not even felt to be able to follow the normal *cursus honorum* of every Roman aristocrat. Thus this strange man, boyishly immature, grew old, ignored and forgotten both by Augustus and Tiberius.

But Claudius was not bereft of abilities. Through many years of study he gained a considerable command of literature and history. And when destiny brought him to the pinnacle of power, despite errors and unpardonable weaknesses he could promulgate important laws, undertake gigantic public works, plan and bring to conclusion grandiose military enterprises. His

23. The portrait of Antonia is reproduced in Plate VII.

24. *Lives of the Twelve Caesars,* 5.4.

internal policies as well were substantially balanced, and had as their end the reestablishment of trust between the princeps and the old senatorial aristocracy which had been so seriously damaged by the insanity of Caligula and above all by his eastward-leaning policy. Nevertheless, both before and after his accession to the throne his weak and immature character, his pliable nature, his fears, his credulity and weakness allowed women and freedmen to use their personality to influence him and to exploit him for their own ends.

After two unhappy marriages which ended in divorce, Claudius had married Valeria Messalina, a young girl of aristocratic background whose family was related to the family of Augustus[25]. To them, in the year 40, there was born a daughter, Octavia, who was to be the unhappy first wife of Nero, and later a son, Britannicus, who was born 20 days after his father's accession to the throne.

25. At the time of their marriage Messalina was only fourteen, while Claudius was thirty-four years older than she.

The Roman sources describe Messalina as a corrupt intriguer, and although Tacitus and Suetonius, like all Roman historians, were much given to recounting gossip, in this case one can hardly doubt their statements. On the other hand, Claudius's particularly abnormal nature must be taken into consideration. His weak and pliable nature throughout his life rendered him prey to his freedmen and wives. It is no wonder, then, that a woman hardly more or less corrupt than so many other Roman matrons of the time abused the unbelievable weaknesses of such a husband, both by profiting from her position as first lady and by giving free rein to her erotic desires.

Messalina's disgraceful conduct lasted seven years. For seven years this young woman sold her influence to allied kings, to contractors of public works, and to rich men who wished to obtain some privilege or favor from imperial authority. And for seven years this income served to feed boundless luxury and unbridled license.

How much Claudius knew and tolerated is one of the mysteries of history. But Roman mentality could not conceive that a man who was unable to govern a woman could govern an empire, and intrigues and plots to overturn the emperor became more and more frequent in Rome.

Of Messalina's last intrigue we know very much and very little at the same time. The man was Gaius Silius, "the handsomest youth in Rome"[26], ambitious and a member of one of the most noble families of the capital. A plot to depose and kill Claudius was organized by Messalina and her young lover. As a prelude to the *coup d'état,* there took place an incredible and inexplicable (at least to our way of thinking) wedding between Silius and Messalina, solemnly celebrated while Claudius was momentarily away from Rome. Neither Suetonius nor Tacitus gives a convincing explanation of this apparent madness which cost the conspirators their lives. Whatever the solution of this enigma, we know the immediate consequences. More through fear of being deposed and killed than from a sense of honor, Claudius allowed himself to be guided once again by the all-powerful freedmen of his court. Silius and the other conspirators were killed immediately. Messalina, who had taken refuge in the garden of Lucullus, was cut down by order of the freedman Narcissus when he saw that Claudius's anger was rapidly receding. She was only twenty-three, and up to the last moment there remained with her her mother Lepida, "who

26. Tacitus, *Annals,* 11.12.

had taken pity on her daughter in her time of trouble though she had quarrelled with her when she was in power" [27].

27. Tacitus, *Annals,* 11.37.

Even the statues of Valeria Messalina were overturned and destroyed throughout the empire, by a decree of the Senate, always servile before the strong and inflexible before the vanquished. There remain only a few coin portraits from provincial Greek cities of the beautiful and corrupt woman who had dominated the society of Rome for so many years. One of these, perhaps the most attractive, is illustrated in Plate XI. The face of Messalina appears here on a large worn bronze coin of Nicaea. Hers is a young face, almost that of an adolescent, and beautiful with a sweet beauty bordering on the pallid. She is the antithesis of what this wife of Claudius should have been, morally if not physically. But even though the hand of the Greek artist may have slightly altered the expression of the face to achieve a calm and typically Greek composition, this head of Messalina is unquestionably a portrait. It is a portrait in which we may examine the precious testimony of the facial traits of this faithless woman. There is nothing more, however, because the author of this portrait could not see beyond external form and has not known how to express that deeper imprint which lies behind the features of a face.

The supreme talent of a portraitist is to express in a wrinkle of the face, in the turn of the mouth, in the expression of a glance, the deeper essence of character and the mark of destiny. It suffices to test this observation in the marvelous portrait of Octavia which is illustrated in Plate II of this book. The coin of Nicaea, despite its impeccable stylistic perfection, gives the features but not the soul of the corrupt great-granddaughter of Octavia [28].

28. Octavia, the sister of Augustus, was in fact the great-grandmother of Messalina. To form a clearer idea of this relationship, one may consult the Julio-Claudian genealogical table, page 4.

The portraits of the woman who succeeded Messalina have a rather different interest, not only artistic but also historical. Although Claudius, already advanced in years and still in shock from the danger he had encountered, told the praetorians that he would never remarry "because his marriages always ended so badly" [29], the invisible congeries of influences which always surrounded and guided him shortly made him change his mind. Once again, a wife was selected for the unwearied emperor and among the intrigues of the freedmen there prevailed those which put forward Agrippina, the last living daughter of Germanicus, whom we have already met portrayed with her two sisters, Julia and Drusilla, on an interesting sestertius of Caligula [30].

29. Suetonius, *Lives of the Twelve Caesars,* 5.26.

30. See Plate X.

In A.D. 49, when Claudius married her [31], Agrippina, as the emperor's niece, was already at home in the imperial house. She was thirty-four years old, widowed and the mother of a son by her first husband, Gnaeus Domitius Ahenobarbus. The eyes and hopes of all men were centered on this boy, in whose veins there ran the blood of the already mythical Germanicus. Intelligent, well-mannered, diffident and shy, rigidly educated in the old way, this boy was named Nero and was twelve years old.

31. Claudius, as the brother of Germanicus, was Agrippina's uncle. It was necessary, therefore, to make a specific exception to matrimonial law which up to then held such a union to be incestuous.

Claudius's new wife was of a quite different temper from Messalina. From her mother, whose name she bore and whose handsome features we illustrate in Plate VIII, she inherited an iron will and endless ambition and probably, in spite of the gossip of Suetonius and Tacitus, her moral character. The influence that this woman exercised on Claudius during the last five years of his reign was enormous. Far more intelligent than Messalina, the daughter of

Germanicus played her cards with detachment and determination. She was a typical representative of the old traditional aristocracy, and used her power not for mean personal ends but to reform the state according to her ideas, which were those of the ancient republican oligarchy. A strong government, bound to the high conservative nobility, of whose power the emperor was only the temporary custodian: this was Agrippina's objective, and Claudius, subjected as ever by a personality stronger than his own, became a docile instrument of this aristocratic restoration. Agrippina, meanwhile, thought of the future. Only a year after her marriage Nero, nearly thirteen years of age, was adopted by the emperor. As for the other heir, Britannicus, the second child of Messalina and Claudius, one could take care of him later. Moreover, he was four years younger than Nero.

The last five years of Claudius's reign marked the triumph of this woman of iron. Never before in Rome had so much power been concentrated in a woman's hands. And that sensitive seismograph of imperial politics, coins, confirms what we already know from the historians. Let us look at an aureus struck at Rome illustrated in Plate XII. While on one face of the coin there is the rather dull face of Claudius, on the other there is the visage of Agrippina. This fact in itself is symptomatic because never before had the emperors permitted their wives the honor of being portrayed on the official coins of the Roman state. A certain reserve, if nothing more than the conception of the imperial office itself, which at this time was still fully understood as the highest office of a republic, had kept the emperors from a step which would have been widely interpreted as ostentation in the style of the Hellenistic monarchs. At the most, toleration was shown when some city of the Eastern empire with Greek servility toward its Roman masters issued coins carrying the portrait of the wife of the princeps. But official Roman coinage was something else again. Not even Augustus had ever allowed Livia the honor of seeing herself portrayed on the coins of the state. And when Tiberius gave this honor to his mother, on the occasion of the high honors decreed by the Senate to the aged widow of Augustus, he had the tact to bestow the youthful features of Livia on the heads of three divinities, Pietas, Iustitia and Salus Augusta [32]. In the same way, a mint magistrate of the time of Augustus was pleased to give the features of Julia, daughter of the emperor, to a bust of Diana [33], while the three sisters of Caligula had appeared on the reverse of a sestertius in the guise of three goddesses, Securitas, Fortuna and Concordia [34].

All portraits of other imperial ladies had been up to this time posthumous and commemorative, for example, that of the elder Agrippina struck on coins by her son Caligula [35] and that of Antonia appearing in the coinage of her son Claudius [36], while the wives of Caligula and Nero, avowed graecophiles, unhindered by any sensitivity towards Roman tradition, had to content themselves with appearances on local coinages issued by far-off Greek cities.

And so Agrippina, who was so rigidly bound to the mentality of the old oligarchs, was the first woman to break through this traditional barrier, a revealing indication of a nature in which there was perpetuated, in an exasperated form, the burning ambition which had tragically marked the lives of her mother and grandmother. Nonetheless, this ambition was halted halfway. In

32. See Plates IV and V.

33. See Chapter 2, "In the House of Augustus: Livia, Antonia and Julia".

34. See Plate X.

35. See Plate VIII.

36. See Plate VII.

fact, we see that the face of the emperor always accompanies the portrait of Agrippina as if to lessen the significance of the innovation. Besides, the portrait of the wife of Claudius appears only on gold and silver; that is, on the coins the emission of which was the exclusive right of the emperor. The head of Agrippina is never seen on an as, a dupondius, or a sestertius. Evidently the Senate, though servile, did not allow this woman's head to appear on the bronze coinage over which it held exclusive prerogative.

But let us return for a moment to our coin. The inscription, AGRIPPINAE AUGUSTAE, which runs around the portrait of Agrippina, is also historically interesting. It confirms that the title "Augusta" was borne by the daughter of Germanicus during the lifetime of her husband, for the first time in the history of the empire [37]. The same title, AGRIPP AUGUSTA, is repeated on a cistophorus [38] of Ephesus which we reproduce in Plate XIII. Here too the portrait of Agrippina is shown as an ever-present shadow behind the massive head of her aging spouse.

37. Among the imperial ladies before Agrippina, only Livia enjoyed this title during her life, and only in her last years, after the death of Augustus.

38. A silver coin commonly struck in the Hellenistic era and then under the Roman empire by various Greek cities of Asia Minor.

Although the importance of these coins as historical documents is enormous, one cannot say as much for them as works of art. We may say, in fact, that neither the aureus struck at Rome nor the cistophorus issued in far-off Ephesus can tell us much from an aesthetic point of view. Roman portraiture has been reduced to a completely different level of representation. The generalized characterization of the portrait on the Eastern cistophorus shown us nothing of what must have been the face of Agrippina. And even the aureus of Rome on which the head of the Augusta is alone and therefore more visible does not add greatly to our identikit. Looking at this face, one has the clear impression of a caricature of facial features completely altering the appearance of the woman. First of all, the eyes are disproportionately large. Then the nose is too pointed and long, the neck is exaggerated and thin, the mouth only sketched. Everything contributes to create an impression of a visage deformed in a hopeless attempt to create an effect. The rudimentary and graceless treatment of the drapery confirms our suspicion that we have before us the work of an artist of modest talent.

Far more convincing is the portrait of Agrippina preserved by a didrachm coined in the Eastern provinces of the empire (Plate XIV). When this coin was struck Claudius was already dead, and the young Nero, having barely acceded to the throne thanks to the maneuvers of his mother, was reigning in name but not in fact, since he was dominated by the iron will of Agrippina. This is, therefore, the crowning moment of the Augusta's power, and the engraver of this exceptional piece seems to have been aware of it. Perhaps without reflecting, his hand which had engraved for the other face of the coin a weak and generalized portrait of the young emperor [39] comes suddenly to life to give us a portrait of the daughter of Germanicus of exceptional expressive power. Once again, an artist succeeds in understanding and expressing in facial features the more profound outlines of a spirit. In the play of light and shade on the high forehead, in the strong and fleshy nose, the swelling lips, and the willful chin, we see all the tenacious inflexibility of the overbearing and dominating character which in a few years will have brought Agrippina to ruin and death. Written around a portrait like this, the banal inscription AGRIPPINA

39. Not illustrated on the plates. The reproduction of the two sides of this coin is included in the Descriptive Index of Coins (page 110).

AUGUSTA MATER AUGUSTI (Agrippina Augusta, Mother of the Augustus) is weighted with portent and significance and has the sound of an overbearing assertion of power. In coins such as this and those that we shall shortly describe one may read, in the synthesis of a few images, the tragic epilogue of the life of this woman which we have already come to know through the powerful pages of Tacitus. What follows the elevation of Nero is in fact at the same time the story of a son rebelling against the too-stern yoke of his mother and of a woman who believes she can continue to exercise the influence which she had over a weak and inept husband over a son who has already become emperor. And, as we have said, the steps of this psychological drama, full of Freudian implications, are revealed for one who can read them in the images of a few significant coins.

Let us look at the aureus shown on Plate XV. This is one of the very first coins of the reign of Nero. The year is A.D. 54. The seventeen-year-old emperor, not yet having reached his majority, is still a docile instrument in the hands of his mother, and this coin shows it fully. On the obverse, around the facing busts of mother and son, there is the legend AGRIPP AUG DIVI CLAUD NERONIS CAES MATER[40], while the titles of the young Nero are confined to the reverse of the coin. It is the first time that this occurs in the history of the empire, and this coin truly marks the height of Agrippina's power. On the reverse, enclosed in an oak crown, there is the large legend EX S C[41], this, too, full of deep political significance. For the first time since the age of Augustus, who had given to the emperor the exclusive right of coining gold and silver, leaving to the Senate only the control of the bronze coinage, this abbreviation reappears on gold and silver coins. And this, too, is a proof of the power of Agrippina, considering that Claudius's widow was the most important defender of Senatorial prestige.

Now let us examine the denarius shown in Plate XVI. The year is A.D. 55; only a few months have gone by, but something has already changed. Nero, eighteen, was already in love with the freedwoman Acte and was openly considering the repudiation of Octavia, the wife his mother had forced on him while still a boy[42]. Agrippina's indignation at such a proposal was great. There was the Lex de Maritandis Ordinibus, which prohibited marriage between a senator and a freedwoman, but apart from this there was the question of a mother's authority for the first time placed in question, and a woman like Agrippina could certainly not tolerate this. We know that there were violent scenes, and that Nero, at least officially , bowed his head. Nevertheless, from that moment on Octavia was neglected and the relation with Acte kept on in a tenacious way known only to what is prohibited. When, thirteen years later, Nero, abandoned by everyone, committed suicide, Acte the freedwoman and former mistress was there to make the final gesture of respect by burying his remains.

This, then, was the first act of a family division that was destined to widen in time, and the coin that we are describing already shows by its portraits and its inscriptions that the star of Agrippina had begun to set. The titles of the Augusta have given way to those of the young emperor and are relegated to the reverse of the coin. The portraits of mother and son are also no longer placed face to face, as in the preceding coin. The profile of Agrippina now appears in

40. AGRIPPINA AUGUSTA DIVI CLAUDII NERONIS CAESARIS MATER, that is to say, Agrippina Augusta, wife of divine Claudius, mother of Nero Caesar.

41. EX SENATUS CONSULTO, that is to say, by decree of the Senate.

42. Octavia was the elder daughter of Messalina and Claudius and sister of Britannicus. At thirteen, in A.D. 53, she had been married to the sixteen-year-old Nero.

the background, behind the head of her young, rebellious son, a barely noticeable sign of the decline soon to become ruinous.

Then everything is seized up in a rapid succession of events and the duel between a man ever more set on governing and living in his own way and the immoderately ambitious woman ready to conspire even against her son rather than lose her power moves toward its tragic conclusion. It will be another woman, however, Poppaea Sabina, with whom Nero fell in love in A.D. 58, who gives the coup de grâce to Agrippina[43]. Poppaea was six years older than the emperor. She was refined, beautiful, loved luxury and life as Julia once had. Hebraiophile and infatuated by the East, by Greece, and in favor, as was Nero, of a populist and anti-senatorial policy, she was thus the natural enemy of Agrippina. She understood clearly that as long as Claudius's widow lived the last glimmer of his former subjugation could not be extinguished in the soul of Nero. The unfortunate Octavia, neglected, abused, was still queen in the imperial palace, and as long as Agrippina lived, Nero did not dare to repudiate her. Thus, in part at the instigation of Poppaea and in part to liberate himself from the tyrannous and frustrating shadow of Agrippina, Nero was brought to the matricide of Baiae.

43. Poppaea, who was twenty-seven years old, had been married shortly before to the twenty-six-year-old senator Otho, one of the short-reigned emperors who succeeded Nero. While at court Otho spoke of his wife in such lyric terms that the emperor requested to make her acquaintance. Shortly afterwards, Poppaea became Nero's mistress. Getting poor Otho out of the way was a simple affair. Although he had never been more than a quaestor, he was sent to govern one of the most distant provinces, remote Lusitania. But the most curious thing is that Otho continued to love his ex-wife, so much so that in A.D. 69, during the brief period of his emperorship, he had her statues, which the people of the capital had pulled down, reerected.

The description of this crime is given in some of the most beautiful pages of the literature of any era. In the clear starry night, the ship which was destined to sink cradles itself on the calm waves while Agrippina and her freedwoman talk without suspicion by the light of the moon. Then the anxiety which betrays the assassins and their abortive maneuvers to sink the ship. On land, meanwhile, the nervous vigil of Nero and the panic which overcomes him when it is reported that Agrippina has swum to safety. Then, in a rapid and implacable chain of events, the nocturnal council with Seneca and Burrus and the long, anguished silence, broken at last by the ambiguous proposal of the philosopher who asks Burrus if his praetorians could carry out the duty at which the sailors failed. And the anxious retreat of Burrus from the terrible responsibility: no, it is not his men (who would refuse to lift their hands against a daughter of Germanicus), but it is the sailors who should conclude the work that they have not finished! Finally, Anicetus and his sailors, hastening at night to a villa in which Agrippina had taken refuge; the door broken down, the eruption into her room, and a hail of daggers. Almost cinematographic sequences, the terrible night which the pen of Tacitus, at a distance of 2000 years, makes alive again before our eyes with a disturbingly modern vigor.

Of Poppaea, the enemy of Agrippina who in a few years would marry Nero, we have only a portrait on a drachma coined by an unknown mint in Asia Minor. We do not know in what degree this is a faithful portrait of the young Roman patrician. However that may be, it is the face of a beautiful and interesting woman with a strong and willful expression. In Plate XVII, we put it side by side with the unmistakable adult portrait of Nero, of Nero now free to follow to the end his propensities, free to govern, to collect, to write poetry, to marry and divorce, to live, even, in a base fashion, but by himself, without the constant and inhibiting reign of his awe-inspiring mother.

# Chapter 3 THE FLAVIANS

## Domitilla, Julia, Domitia: Light and Shade in the House of Vespasian.

With the death of Nero, who killed himself June 9, A.D. 68, the Julio-Claudian dynasty was extinguished after a century of power. Following the tragic period of civil wars after the death of the thirty-one-year-old emperor, there emerged towards the end of 69 the strong figure of an old general, Vespasian. Son of a tax-collector, born at Rieti in the Sabine territory, the new emperor belonged to that Italian middle class which for decades had furnished the state its new civilian and military administrators. With him the whole class of the prosperous Italian bourgeoisie gained consciousness of its role in the life of the state, entered and revitalized the Senate, and mingled with the old aristocracy of the capital.

Even at court a new spirit emerged, just as the excesses, intrigues, and perversions of the last thirty years reached a height. The bourgeois virtues of moderation and of thrifty respectability were rediscovered by a society satiated with intrigues and vices. And this stamp put on the decade of his reign by the new emperor was to be conserved, excepting the period of Domitian, for more than a century.

When Vespasian came to power he was sixty years old and a widower. With notable good sense, he did not wish to remarry. He preferred to take as a concubine an elderly freedwoman who could not interfere excessively in affairs of state. And after she died, in A.D. 75, the women who succeeded her were more housekeepers than mistresses and never had any power.

We have little information concerning Vespasian's wife, Flavia Domitilla, who had borne him his two sons, Titus and Domitian, and a daughter, who also died when Vespasian was still an obscure civilian. Suetonius mentions her briefly, giving the information that before marrying the future emperor she was the mistress of Statilius Capella, a Roman knight of Sabratha in Africa. He further adds that originally she enjoyed only Latin citizenship, but that she became a full Roman citizen following a court case brought by her father Flavius Liberalis of Ferentinum, a mere quaestor's secretary [1]. More we do not know, but all the same we have excellent coin portraits of this shadowy and prematurely deceased woman on a few rare coins that Titus, assuming the emperorship after the death of Vespasian, had coined out of filial piety in honor of the mother who had died so many years before.

1. Suetonius, *Lives of the Twelve Caesars,* 8 Vespasian 3.

Let us look at the denarius in Plate XVIII. Domitilla's is a still youthful face, but fleshy and matronly and supported by a solid neck. The strand of beads, the complex and artful hairdressing, rather similar to that adopted by Agrippina in the splendid portrait we illustrate in Plate XIV, are not able to refine the rather common look of the subject. In spite of the elegant hairstyling, in spite of the jewelry, and in spite of the impressive title of Augusta due the wife and mother of emperors, in this posthumous portrait Domitilla still has the placid and well-fed look of the housewife she must have had when she was the spouse of a minor provincial functionary. This is basically the same air that we find in the coin portrait of her husband (Plate XIX), the solid look of a bourgeois, of peasant background, attached to the land and to memories of his origins, no matter to what height fortune may have raised him. Suetonius speaks almost with affection of these bourgeois sentiments of the old Vespasian. "He was brought up in the country under the guidance of his maternal grandmother and, because of this, even as emperor he often returned to the place of his childhood, having left the villa just as it was in order not to change anything that his eye fixed in his memory. And he had such veneration for the memory of his grandmother that on festive and solemn days he always continued to drink from her little silver cup" [2]. Domitilla too would probably have had her share of such gentle and intimate sentiments if fate had allowed her to grow old beside her husband.

2. Suetonius, *Lives of the Twelve Caesars,* 8 Vespasian 2.

The elder son of Vespasian, Titus, had a brief reign. Widowed in his first marriage and divorced by a second wife before his father became emperor, during the long war of the Jewish revolt he had become intimate with a middle-aged Jewish woman fully thirteen years older than he. Julia Berenice, daughter of King Agrippa the First, born in A.D. 28, was rich and corrupt. She had married twice before becoming the mistress of her brother, Agrippa II. This "Cleopatra in miniature", as Mommsen defines her, came to Rome twice, probably with the secret hope that Titus would marry her, the first time in A.D. 75 and then again in A.D. 79, when Vespasian died and Titus inherited the empire. On both occasions, perhaps because of the violent opposition of the people, her hopes were disappointed [3].

3. Suetonius, speaking of Titus, says concisely, "He immediately sent Berenice away from the city, although both of them were sad" (*Lives of the Twelve Caesars,* 8 Titus 7).

By his second wife, Marcia Furnilla, Titus had a daughter famous for her beauty and her elegance, whose tragic destiny was entwined with that of her uncle Domitian and his wife Domitia Longina. For reasons unknown to us, during the brief reign of Titus, the girl, who must have been still very young, was proposed repeatedly as a bride to her uncle Domitian, but he refused to marry his young niece. In order to do this he would have had to divorce Domitia Longina, whom he had persuaded to abandon her husband and come live with him in his youth, during the reign of his father. Later he had married her and had by her a child who died in infancy.

The story of the last of the Flavians is inextricably bound to this woman, who was destined to rule him throughout her life by her charm and who in the end was fatal to him. After her husband's ascent to the throne, Domitia did not try to influence political affairs. However, in spite of Domitian's numerous love affairs, she always knew how to use an irresistible physical attraction over him. Daughter of Corbulo, the famous general who had been victim of the Neronian purges, Domitia had a troubled life. Shortly after her husband's assumption of power she had an affair with a dancer named Paris. She was discovered and sent into exile, while her lover was executed, but after only two years Domitian, who could not do without her, called her back and pardoned her. Such clemency cost the emperor dearly, because in A.D. 96 his formidable wife was among those who wove the plot that cost him his life.

In the private life of the last of the Flavians there is entwined the sad story of his relations with his niece Julia. We do not know why Titus had given Domitian the opportunity of marrying his daughter. However, subsequent events, the submissiveness with which Julia yielded to seduction by her uncle, and their long, bitter affair perhaps offer a logical explanation. The Flavians, after all, had never been part of the Roman aristocracy. Their customs and their manner of thinking were that of the provincial middle classes which did not completely avoid sentiment and did not completely subordinate the reasoning of the heart to the cold strategy of marriage alliances as did the Roman aristocracy. How many young girls had not chanced to fall in love with a "grownup" uncle, at least for a few months? Perhaps this may have happened to the young Julia, and Titus, with no ulterior motive but only yielding to the burning desire of the daughter whom he so dearly loved, repeatedly asked Domitian to marry the girl. Domitian, as we have seen, refused, but only, like the libertine he was, to seduce his niece, after she had married someone else, and Julia docilely agreed to become the mistress of a man who had refused her as a wife.

The affair, begun while Titus was still alive, went on after the death of the emperor. The inconvenient husband, Titus Flavius Sabinus, was put to death, and when Domitia was sent into exile Julia began to live openly with Domitian and perhaps hoped finally to take the place of his unfaithful wife. But once more fate was against her. Having undergone the humiliation of seeing Domitia return to Rome and renew a bond of marriage which had seemed forever broken, the daughter of Titus found herself pregnant. Domitian forced her to have an abortion and Julia died, still very young.

The coin portraits of the ill-fated granddaughter of Vespasian do not do her justice. Statues and cameos show us a beautiful and refined woman wearing complicated hairstyles. The taste of the period demanded buxom women and in all her portraits Julia conforms. However, there is a recurrent factor in the coin portraits of the daughter of Titus. From coin to coin, her expression and her features vary so much that, by using the coins alone (as is usual in iconographic research) it would be hard to reconstruct the true features of this woman. Therefore, we illustrate the only coin of Julia that has iconographical interest. The dupondius reproduced in Plate XX was minted between 80 and 81, during the reign of Titus. The inscription, IULIA IMP T AUG F AUGUSTA[4], in which the initial of Titus is not preceded by the adjective "divine", shows us that the emperor was still alive.

How old was Julia between 80 and 81? Twelve or thirteen, no more. The passion for her thirty-year-old uncle which would change her life in such a tragic way began then in her adolescent mind. Even if among the Romans, as among all southern people, women matured rather early, the face of this coin is still the fat and insignificant countenance of a little girl. Her complicated hairstyle, the first of those fantastic and complicated hairdos adopted by Julia during her short life, does not make her look grown up. Her hair is divided by a long transverse part from ear to ear; the hair of the back of her head is pulled back and tied tightly at the nape of her neck in a soft clump of thick curls; the rest of her hair forms an impressive mass of very small curls which crown her temples and her forehead. This is the hairdo that, as it evolves, in a short time

4. IULIA IMPERATORIS TITI AUGUSTI FILIA AUGUSTA, that is, Julia Augusta, daughter of Titus, emperor Augustus.

leads to incredible architectural constructions of such complication and artificiality as to make the most sophisticated eighteenth-century hairdos insignificant in comparison. But aside from the interesting hairdo, and aside from the sense of pain which the portrait of this unfortunate adolescent provokes in those who know her tragic history, this coin is also important for another reason: for the first time, a living woman of the imperial family is shown alone on an official Roman coin. This is not all; Julia's face appears not only on pieces of gold and silver emitted by the imperial government but also, as our coin shows, on a bronze dupondius emitted by the Senate. Time has not passed without change. The honor which only thirty years before had been denied to an exceptional woman like Agrippina[5] is now conceded to a twelve-year-old Augusta. In a few years Domitian was to proclaim himself lord and god, *Dominus et Deus.* The Republican time is now far off and forgotten.

5. See Chapter 2, "The Women of Claudius and Nero: Messalina, Agrippina, Poppaea".

We offer the reader portraits of the other woman in the life of Domitian, Domitia Longina, and of her consort in Plate XXI. Quite possibly there does not exist in all Roman iconography a couple as odious in appearance as this. All the ill-will of the senatorial class for the last of the Flavians seems to be concentrated in the exceptional portrait of Domitian which an unknown master has cut for this coin. The widespread habit of certain Roman engravers of accentuating facial characteristics of imperial personages represented on coins to the point of the grotesque with the intention of giving them a better characterization is here only an excuse. The menacing eye burrowed under the heavy arch of the eyebrow, the hooked nose of a predator, the upper lip hooked over the twisted mouth, altogether make the portrait struck in silver on this coin the repugnant image of a degenerate. And whatever the art historian may think of it, only hatred and terror could have guided the hand of the author of this work.

The face of Domitia shown on the aureus illustrated on the same plate is less fearsome and bestial, but just as cold and hateful. Below a complicated hair arrangement which could even be a wig, there appears the heavy and capricious face of a virago to whom the engraver, out of spite, has given the same features as Domitian. The eye, the unmistakable nose, the chin and the heavy bone structure of the face are almost identical in both portraits. It follows that the face of the Augusta takes on, in the eye of the observer, an equivocal unnatural element which makes one think more of a transvestite than a woman. It is certainly possible that Domitia Longina was not beautiful. Fascination is not necessarily connected to physical appearance. But a woman who dominated a sensual nature such as that of Domitian for twenty-five years cannot have been as repulsive as our coin would have us believe.

Looking at these pieces, one must really ask oneself how such disrespectful engravers could have carried on their work without arousing the anger of the authorities. But this also is one of the small and large enigmas that the study of Roman coins keeps in store for those who cultivate it.

Chapter 4

# THE HEIGHT OF THE EMPIRE

## Plotina, Marciana, Matidia, Sabina: the Proper Ladies of Trajan and Hadrian.

On September 16, A.D. 96, Domitian, the last emperor of the Flavian house, fell under the daggers of conspirators.

After the brief reign of the elderly Nerva, there ascended to the throne on January 25, A.D. 98, Marcus Ulpius Trajanus, a general who was extremely popular among the western legions and the man whom Nerva himself had adopted as heir shortly before he died.

The new emperor had been born forty-four years earlier at Italica in southern Spain. Now for the first time a provincial reached the throne, thus crowning the political and social evolution of decades. In the nineteen years of his reign and in the twenty-one years of the principate of his relative and successor Hadrian, the power of the empire reached its peak. Thereafter, slowly and almost imperceptibly at first, then more rapidly and ruinously, there began the decline of the Roman world.

Few natures were at the same time so diverse and complementary as those of Trajan and Hadrian. The first was an able and efficient soldier, a stranger by nature to all barren intellectualism, who was able to give the empire its last great expansionistic impulse, extending its borders to limits never reached before or after. The second was an intellectual, Hellenist to the marrow, who dedicated his inexhaustible traveller's energy to becoming the first emperor to visit every part of the immense dominions of Rome. His tireless travelling almost always led to understanding the problems of individual provinces, providing for them, reorganizing, restructuring, sometimes even courageously rectifying the borders of the boundless empire, and making the citizens of the most remote provinces understand for the first time that the Roman state, more than a political unity, was, beyond and above the languages and customs of the individual people, a powerful spiritual unity destined to endure for centuries. Thus, the forty-year combined reigns of the conqueror of the Dacians and the Parthians[1] and of the restorer of the world, *restitutor orbis*[2], carried the Roman state to the apogee of its long parabola, making of the empire the most grandiose and homogeneous territorial, political and social unity in the history of all time[3].

The bonds between the strikingly different personalities of these two great emperors were four women whose portraits have been conserved through the centuries by rare and interesting coins. These were Plotina and Marciana, wife and sister respectively of Trajan, Matidia, daughter of Marciana and therefore niece of the warrior emperor, and Sabina, daughter of Matidia, who was married by Plotina when she was barely twelve years old to the twenty-four-year-old Hadrian, son of a first cousin of Trajan's. We know very little about these four women who must have been well-defined personalities and, at least in one case, played an important role in the destiny of the empire.

1. For his remarkable victories over the Dacians of King Decebalus and the Parthians of Pacorus Trajan gained the title of Dacicus and Parthicus from the Senate.

2. Hadrian was also called restorer of the world for the many public works (roads, baths, temples, bridges, aqueducts) which he generously and systematically financed in all the provinces and cities he visited during his long reign.

3. In modern times there have been empires like the English and the Spanish larger in extent than the Roman empire. But they have always consisted of colonial dominions over which a relatively small nation politically and economically dominated vast areas outside of Europe which were not socially integrated with the colonizer. Among the provinces of the Roman empire, on the other hand, there was territorial continuity and political and social homogeneity.

After the disquieting but powerful voice of Tacitus is stilled and the anecdotal and gossiping but always interesting voice of Suetonius has ceased, an almost total silence envelops the imperial ladies of the second century. The chapters dealing with this period by the writer nearest to the events, the Greek historian Cassius Dio, have reached us in a very fragmentary state. Beyond him, we must content ourselves with a few dim epitomators of the later empire, with epigraphical material that is always problematical and uncertain, and with those well-known lives of the *Historia Augusta* that are nonetheless compilations of a late age and in which it is extremely difficult to discern the few noteworthy pieces of information among the mountains of obscene gossip and absurd tales.

Immersed in this thick cloud, figures lose solidity and become dim, evanescent shadows. In place of the ardent passions of the women of the first century and the burning court tragedies inimitably described by the hand of Tacitus, there is now a calm and cold expanse of cloud. A few bits of information emerge like isolated rocks, sufficient to make us feel that had the Roman world of the second century produced another Tacitus capable of telling their story, Plotina, Marciana, Matidia and Sabina would live in our imagination with a prominence equal to that of Livia, Antonia, Agrippina and the other great women of the first century. This necessary preface made, we may now examine the personages and the portraits of the four Augustas who accompanied the earthly adventures of Trajan and Hadrian. First of all, Plotina. The ancient sources give us few items of information about her, and those are contradictory. The younger Pliny praises her and calls her "sanctissima foemina" (revered lady). Cassius Dio, on the other hand, refers to her senile passion for Hadrian and retails the gossip that circulated about the presumed poisoning of Trajan by his wife. Infidelity and poisoning!

But how many times were these identical accusations hurled with exasperating monotony at the members of the imperial family? The senatorial class, longing for its ancient powers, exercised itself in the centuries of the empire in sharpening and applying venom to this defamatory and infamous technique of slander directed against the emperors and their families. No human sympathy remained unstained by foul calumny, and in every important or premature death they wished to see the sinister effect of poison [4].

On the contrary, there is absolutely nothing strange in the fact that the intellectual Hadrian was liked and respected by a cultivated and intelligent woman like Plotina [5]. Plotina herself confirmed this honest affection by arranging the marriage between Hadrian and the young Sabina and thus knitting together the bonds of relationships which already existed between the emperor and his youngest cousin. Trajan, too, had a certain admiration, if not liking, for Hadrian, so much so that when he felt his death approaching, he left Hadrian to govern Syria, the most sensitive and important region of the empire at that moment [6].

There are no real reasons, therefore, to label Plotina an adulteress and poisoner. On the contrary, her long harmonious life with Trajan, her modesty, revealed in anecdotes told even by her most wily detractors, her habit of accompanying the emperor in his warlike enterprises, which remained an

4. Gaius and Lucius, grandsons of Augustus, the elder Drusus, the brother of Tiberius, Germanicus, the emperor Claudius and his son Britannicus may all have been poisoned, according to the more or less veiled insinuations of Suetonius and Tacitus. Their murderers would have been Livia, Augustus, Tiberius, Caligula, Agrippina the Younger, and Nero. But considering the logic of the facts, the only one of these deaths that can be attributed with some probability to poison is that of the very young Britannicus.

5. We know, in fact, that Plotina was interested in religion and philosophy and showed a certain preference for Epicurean doctrines.

6. In A.D. 116-117, Syria was the trouble spot of the empire. The massive and bloody revolt of the Jews was probably a prelude to the counterattack of the recently defeated Parthians.

attractive characteristic of empresses of this century, make this woman a great historical figure completely worthy of the greatest Roman tradition. It is not important for us to know whether Hadrian was in fact adopted by the dying Trajan or whether Plotina, interpreting a will he was unable to express, sanctioned the accession of Hadrian by her own authoritative testimony. Only one thing is sure. With providential readiness and determination, this strong and wise woman knew how to support, and perhaps also how to bring about, a choice which was to show itself particularly fortunate for the empire.

Now let us look at the face of this new Livia as shown on the coins minted in her honor. On the aureus of Plate XXII the wife of Trajan appears with a hard and experienced face, like a faded woman of middle age. It is the same expression found in the bust in the Capitoline Museum, and the austere seriousness of this face is somewhat emphasized by the complicated and majestic hairdo that rises like a complex building on the head of the empress. Secured by a ribbon tied above her forehead, her hair swells in a high soft wave pushed back by a rich diadem. Behind this high ornament, her long locks divided into numerous slender tresses reach to her back where, bending back again upwards, they are bound in a tight bun at the nape of her neck. This is the typical hairdo "alla Plotina", one of the many artificial and contorted hairstyles that had become very fashionable among Roman matrons from the time of Julia and Domitia. In this period not one hair, not one curl is allowed to fall naturally. Under the hands of expert hairdressers, baroque constructions are raised higher and with greater complexity on the heads of women. "A globe of hair", says Martial, and Juvenal mocks the new fashion "Stories upon stories were built on her proud head: look at her from the front: she is Andromache. But from behind she is half as tall, and you could believe her another woman!"[7]

We do not know whether these masterpieces were destroyed every night and recreated every morning by patient slave women[8]. However, it is easy to suppose that in this age, as in the eighteenth century, wigs knew their moment of glory. Even a century before, Ovid, in *The Art of Love,* tells us that wigs and toupées were common at Rome. The silky blonde locks of German slave women were desired by Roman brunettes, and mountains of ebony-colored locks came from India, in such a quantity that the imperial government included "Indian hair" among the wares subject to customs duties[9].

The toilette of the high-ranking Roman ladies was in this period, as at the height of the eighteenth century, of a complexity that strains the imagination. If our coins could show us not only the form but also the colors of the faces and the hairdos of the Augustae of this period, the impression would be really striking. The locks were often bleached with the *sapo* of Mainz, a dye obtained by mixing goat fat and beech ashes[10]. Then, having removed their mistress' facial hair, the tireless *ornatrices* had to make her up or rather to "paint" her in white, with gypsum and white lead, on the arms and on the forehead; in red, with ochre or *fucus,* or dregs of wine, on the cheeks and lips; in black, with powdered antimony or simple soot (*fuligo*) on the lashes and around the eyes[11]. With ferocious sarcasm, Martial commented: "Placed among these little pots, your face seems to sleep apart from you"[12].

7. Juvenal, *Satires* 6.502-503.

8. Called *ornatrices* (decorators).

9. *Digest,* 39:4,16, 7.

10. For this *sapo,* see Pliny, *Natural History* 28.191, and Martial, *Epigrams* 14.26.

11. All these operations are described with gusto in the *Epigrams* of Martial, in the *Art of Love* of Ovid, and in the *Satires* of Juvenal.

12. Martial, *Epigrams* 9.37.

We have another splendid portrait of Plotina on an exceptional coin which reunites the faces of the three great personalities of the epoch: Trajan, Hadrian and Plotina herself. This is an aureus coined between A.D. 134 and 138, that is, during the reign of Hadrian (Plate XXV). A new proof of the bond that had united these three people in life is the fact that while Hadrian's profile occupies the obverse of the coin, the heads of Trajan and his wife appear facing each other on the reverse. Around the unmistakable profile of the couple runs the inscription DIVIS PARENTIBUS (to the deified parents), treated with a completely Roman realism, in which the adjective "divis" shows that when this beautiful coin was minted both Trajan and his wife were dead and deified. We know that Plotina probably died in 121, four years after the death of her husband, and that the grateful Hadrian gave her very great honors. Hymns were composed to her, a temple dedicated to her and to Trajan was built in the Forum, and another temple was consecrated to her in Egypt. Nimes, the city of her birth, built a large basilica and dedicated it to her.

On the other face of this beautiful coin (Plate XXV below) the hellenizing and idealized portrait of Hadrian seems almost to synthesize the solar Hellenism of the great emperor in the warm brightness of the gold.

Two other women lived with Plotina in the imperial palace, Marciana, a sister of Trajan, and her daughter Matidia. As Livia and Antonia had lived together a century before, now Plotina, Marciana and Matidia lived in affectionate concord. The same bonds of loyal and long-lasting friendship that had bound the mother-in-law and daughter-in-law in the age of Augustus were renewed in the time of Trajan between the two sisters-in-law and the niece. If we knew nothing else about these women, this perfect accord and total lack of opposition between in-laws which is so rare even in ordinary families would be enough to prove the good sense and the intelligent modesty of the Augustae of Trajan's family [13]. Like Antonia a century before, Marciana and Matidia lived at court and, like Antonia, Matidia, as a widow, remained devoted to the memory of her husband and did not remarry, a rather rare example of devotion among the aristocratic ladies of ancient Rome.

The powerful realistic portraits of these two virtuous women meet us on the coins that Trajan in his fondness for his relatives had minted in their names. On both pieces, a denarius (Plate XXIII) and an aureus (Plate XXIV), both issued after the death and deification of Marciana [14], the first thing that strikes the observer is the strong resemblance between mother and daughter. The depth of the eyesockets, the strong noses, the very harsh cutting of the mouth and chin are identical. Even the hairstyles, another attractive example of the fashion of the times, are substantially the same. The hair is raised over the forehead like a diadem, either thickly entwined, as in the portrait of Matidia (Plate XXIV), or in a triple row of big curls, as in the image of Marciana (Plate XXIII). Then, behind a high diadem that acts to support such elaborate constructions, the long spirals of the curls twist around each other sinuously on the back of the head.

Marciana died about A.D. 112, some five years before her brother, and Matidia continued as long as she lived to be the affectionate friend of Plotina. When Matidia died in A.D. 119 [15], it was Hadrian, made emperor two years before,

13. Plotina and Marciana together gained the title of Augusta in 105. Matidia obtained it after the death of her mother in 112. For the first time, the sisters and the niece of an emperor received the title which previously had been reserved for the mothers, the wives and sometimes the daughters of the emperors.

14. Around the face of Marciana (Plate XXIII) runs the inscription DIVA AUGUSTA MARCIANA (deified Augusta Marciana), while around the head of Matidia (Plate XXIV) the legend is as follows: MATIDIA AUG DIVAE MARCIANAE F (Matidia Augusta, daughter of the deified Marciana).

15. Plotina was to die a few years later, around A.D. 121-122.

who composed her *laudatio funebris*: "Exceedingly dear to her husband, condemned to a long widowhood in the prime of life, she had the wisdom to maintain her purity despite her great beauty. She was helpful to all, troublesome or injurious to none."[16] These are noble words that show that the emperor, whatever his relations with his wife, always maintained an affectionate respect for his mother-in-law.

16. CIL, vol. 14, 3579.

Finally, there is Sabina, the daughter of Matidia, the last of the four ladies of the family of Trajan. She was married when hardly twelve years old to the twenty-three-year-old Hadrian, and it is probable that a wall of reciprocal misunderstanding soon divided her from her husband and his aesthetic tastes. If such infelicity did exist as it appears, the spreaders of libel, always hungry for scandal, exaggerated it to the dimensions of a true conjugal tragedy. Their accounts of the collision between husband and wife arising from Sabina's resentment at the sordid erotic life of the emperor was colored by dramatic accents culminating in the poisoning of Sabina by Hadrian as he became ever more a slave of his homosexual tendencies.

This is the story handed down by the sources. But only a little reflection is sufficient to make one understand how in this case too the scandalous fancy of the Romans, united with the pro-Senatorial historians' aversion to the emperor, have once again distorted reality, transforming a disagreement, no matter how deep, into a bloody melodrama.

In fact, as inscriptions testify[17], Sabina was not only the faithful companion of Hadrian on almost all his travels, but even accompanied her husband on the famous trip to Egypt during which the emperor founded a city in honor of his favorite Antinous. On that luxurious autumn cruise that made its way up the calm waters of the Nile as far as Thebes, there were Hadrian, Sabina, and Antinous himself. As far as the accusation of poison, it is completely improbable that the emperor, by now old, ill, tormented by dropsy, was so much caught up in his unorthodox passions that he would think of eliminating a wife with whom, for better or worse, he had lived for a good thirty-six years.

17. CIG, 4725-4730.

Sabina, as far as we can tell, was not a beautiful woman. The coin portraits that we show in this book offer us two different images, probably made at two different times in her life. In the portrait that appears on the large bronze sestertius shown in Plate XXVI, Sabina has a full, rather fat face with the harsh and austere expression typical of all the women of her family, including Plotina. For the first time, after the follies of the last fifty years, the hairstyle of an empress appears a little simplified, while maintaining a high level of refinement. Held by a narrow circlet, the hair, raised in a pompadour above the forehead, descends on the neck in a sort of large, soft mass. Otherwise, in the other portrait of Sabina, on the aureus reproduced on Plate XXVII above, the locks of the empress appear dressed in one of the most elegant and splendid hairdos seen on Roman coins. But although the hairstyle is structurally the same as we have admired on the coin portraits of Marciana and Matidia, the complex artificiality of the mother's style is loosened into a refined elegance in which the natural beauty of a mass of hair finally prevails over the complicated baroque ideas of the hairdressers. Under her locks, Sabina's face now appears thinner and aged. Her long nose has been sharpened by the years, the cutting of her mouth has become harsher and colder. An inexpressible sense of acrid boredom, a *taedium vitae,* tiredness of life, by now unavoidable, shows from every line of this face.

On the same plate, below, another splendid aureus shows us the willful profile of the man whom reasons of state on a far-off day thirty-six years before had placed forever at her side, Hadrian.

# Chapter 5

# THE ANTONINES

## Mother and Daughter: the Two Faustinas and their Husbands, Antoninus and Marcus Aurelius.

Like the marriage of Trajan and Plotina, that of Hadrian and Sabina was sterile. Once again the Roman state escaped the dangers of a hereditary succession. The method of adoption that had given such good results from the time of Nerva remained the only means of giving a ruler to the immense empire.

And so, in A.D. 138, a few months before his death, Hadrian adopted Antoninus, a man of fifty-two from a very good and wealthy family. Under the rule of the new emperor the Roman state lived through the last long period of splendor and tranquillity in its history.

At the moment of his elevation to the throne, in A.D. 138, Antoninus was married to the beautiful Annia Galeria Faustina, a dozen years his junior, who came from a well-placed provincial family of high political figures and administrators. Around 130, a daughter was born who received her mother's name. She would later become the capricious and sophisticated wife of Marcus Aurelius, her first cousin[1] and the designated heir to the throne[2].

These two women, whom we shall henceforth call Faustina the Elder and Faustina the Younger, had a destiny different and yet in many respects similar. The former, carried away by death at the age of forty-three, enjoyed her electrifying role as first lady of the empire for only three years. The latter, first as daughter and then as wife of an emperor, was for thirty years the most courted and admired woman in Rome, and we too have an echo of her spirited and refined elegance in the imaginative and sophisticated hairdos that crowned her face on coin portraits. Both the mother and the daughter, however, had an extremely fortunate married life. Unlike the unfortunate Sabina, they were literally adored by their respective husbands, covered with honors in their life, and solemnly deified after death.

Honored with the title of Augusta at the time of her husband's elevation to the emperorship, the elder Faustina immediately obtained the right of being portrayed on coins. When she died she was deified. The other imperial ladies who had immediately preceded her, Plotina, Marciana, Matidia and Sabina, had also had this posthumous recognition. But the apotheosis of Faustina was particularly solemn, as if the widowed emperor wished to include his own profound grief in the magnificence of the celebration. The body was buried in the mausoleum of Hadrian[3], and in the temple erected in her honor priestesses of Diva Faustina Augusta celebrated the cult of the new goddess[4]. To honor her memory, there was also created a foundation intended to furnish dowries for poor girls of the city, who were called *Puellae Faustinianae,* Faustina's Girls. Finally, in memory of the divinized empress, there were issued an enormous quantity of coins and on these we can admire her portrait.

1. Marcus Aurelius was in fact the son of Marcus Annius Verus, brother of the elder Faustina.

2. Hadrian, on adopting Antoninus, had imposed on him the duty of adopting in turn as his successors Marcus Aurelius and Lucius Verus, who at Hadrian's death was only eight years old. The latter was the son of that Lucius Ceionius Commodus (on coins, Lucius Aelius Caesar) who was chosen as heir to the empire by Hadrian in 136 but who died before Hadrian in 138. Since Lucius Ceionius Commodus was an inept good-for-nothing and his son was only a child, many historians explain such inexplicable favors with the hypothesis that Lucius Ceionius Commodus was Hadrian's illegitimate son.

3. Today Castel Sant'Angelo.

4. The temple of Diva Faustina still stands. Dedicated in the first instance to her alone, later, after the death of Antoninus, the dedication was extended to her husband as well. The building survived intact to be transformed into the church of San Lorenzo in Miranda in the seventh or eighth century. Its colonnaded facade still stands beside the Sacra Via and on the architrave it is still possible to read the original dedications.

On gold (Plate XXVIII above) and on bronze (Plate XXIX) the wife of Antoninus Pius appears as she must have been in the last years of her life, a middle-aged lady with a matronly and slightly fleshy face. On the aureus shown in Plate XXVIII, the dead empress has her head veiled, while on the sestertius of Plate XXIX she appears with her head uncovered. It is in the refined and complex hairstyle of Faustina that one seems to sense the attention of a distinguished engraver. While the profile of the head (done in very low relief on the coin) is executed graphically rather than by relief, with a swift and sure touch which entrusts the effect of the images more to the firm line of the eye, nose and mouth than to the plastic interplay of light and shade typical of the high-relief coins of this period, the hairdressing of the Augusta is executed with minute care. Parted over the forehead in soft waves, the hair flows down to the nape of the neck. From this point, drawn together in many small braids, it is brought up again to the top of the head where the same braids make a large, soft knot in the form of a ring. Following the artificial creations of the time of Domitia, Plotina and Matidia, one cannot deny that the hairdressing of the elder Faustina, even in its conscious elegance, has greater sobriety and depends less on display and is better proportioned to the dimensions of the face. In looking at the mother's portraits, we already know those of her daughter whose expensive taste is shown in numerous different hairstyles[5], all elegant and refined but at the same time far from the incredibly baroque hair creations in vogue a half-century before.

5. Seven, to be exact.

The adored only daughter of an emperor, wife in her turn of a prince, and not only of a prince but above all of a man of intelligence, cultivation, sensitivity and understanding, Faustina the Younger was a woman indulged by fortune, as seems to be reflected in the coin portraits of her which have survived.

"I would prefer exile with her on Gyaros to a life without her in the palace"[6], Antoninus confessed on one occasion, writing to his friend Fronto. And the honors that Faustina received while still very young are proof of that paternal affection.

6. A small and deserted island of the Cyclades.

Having married at fifteen years of age the heir-designate Marcus Aurelius, in A.D. 147 she gave birth to the first of a long series of children. As a mark of satisfaction at this happy event, Antoninus associated Marcus Aurelius with him in the government while his daughter, hardly seventeen years old, attained the title Augusta and the right to be portrayed on coins. From these happy years of youth, we have the two splendid coin portraits illustrated in Plates XXX and XXXII below. The daughter of Antoninus appears young and beautiful, with that slightly frivolous and indulged air that is typical of those who have had too easy a life. The extroverted character of the young Augusta is already revealed in the splendid hairstyles of these first coin issues. In the portrait illustrated in Plate XXXII, two wide, soft bands of undulating hair descend along the temples and then come together with other strands on the nape of the neck where they fall in a softly developed mass of curls. On the other coin, illustrated in Plate XXX, the hair of the princess appears as it does on a bust of the Capitoline Museum, disposed in flat and regular waves which cover the forehead and the temples to come together again behind the nape of the neck in a rich chignon of fine braids. One larger braid, or perhaps a double strand of beads, encloses the head of the princess like a diadem, elegantly breaking the regular rhythm of the waves of the hairstyle.

7. To Venus Genetrix.

On the reverse of the same coin (Plate XXX below) there appears a draped female figure and around her the legend VENERI GENETRICI[7]. The figure of the goddess of fertility and the legend surrounding it are intended to celebrate the safe delivery of the young bride. The exceptional fertility of the couple who every year were blessed with a new birth must have been taken universally as a good omen. Everyone at court remembered Trajan and Plotina, Hadrian and Sabina, and the long years in which sterility had lain like a curse over the imperial house. In those happy days, no one thought that such fecundity would one day create Commodus, a monster destined to govern tragically and tragically die.

On the death of Antoninus in A.D. 161 power passed to Marcus Aurelius. The long period of calm that characterized the reign of his predecessor had hidden from all eyes the storm that was gathering beyond the borders of the empire to the east and west. While the Persians broke their truce by invading Armenia and Syria, the Huns thousands of kilometers away in another part of the world were driven from their ancient territories in Mongolia by the armies of the Chinese Han dynasty and began a march westward in an attempt to open a path to new lands. Across the steppes of Siberia and the plains of Russia, the wave of invasion pushed westward the populations that it found in its path. And through the Sarmatians, Vendi and Bastarni, the force of this gigantic movement of peoples finally reached the Germans, dislodging them and sending them in turn against the borders of the Roman empire. In 167 the Danubian frontier was attacked and broken by the tribes of the Hermunduri, Marcomanni, Quadi, and the Jazyges, flanked by Longobards and Vandals, two peoples whom the Romans had not encountered before. The hordes broke into the area of Venice and reached Aquileia before being halted. Not since the distant time when Marius had defeated the Cimbri and the Teutons had there been a German invasion of Roman territory. No one could grasp the fact, but that wild incursion was the prelude of a demographic earthquake that was to last for centuries and bring the empire to destruction.

8. Today Sryemska Mitrovica, in Yugoslavia.

9. The Syrian Avidius Cassius, governor of Syria, rebelled in 175 and was recognized as princeps not only in his province but also in Egypt. He was, however, assassinated.

In this juncture of menacing events Faustina was, as far as we can tell, always beside her husband. We find her at Sirmium on the Sava[8] together with Marcus Aurelius during the years of the wars against the Germans, and after the victory over the Quadi the courageous empress, who preferred the zone of operations to the tranquillity of Rome, was acclaimed "Mater Castrorum" (Mother of the Garrisons) by the troops. And when Marcus left for the east to confront the revolt of one of his generals, Faustina went with him[9].

Death overtook her on that very journey, in a distant village of Cappadocia by the name of Halala. It was in the year A.D. 176 and the empress was slightly more than forty-six years old.

10. *Historia Augusta,* Life of Lucius Verus, 10.

Faustina was beautiful, elegant, and lucky. Too fortunate, in fact, to escape the obscene slanderous fantasy of Roman society. The *Historia Augusta*[10] relates that she was the mistress of her son-in-law, Lucius Verus, and more than that, it was Faustina who eliminated him later with a dish of poisoned oysters to avenge herself on him for having confessed his illicit relation to his wife. In

11. *Historia Augusta,* Life of Marcus Aurelius, 19.

another of the *Vitae*[11], we find that the empress chose her lovers from sailors and gladiators at Gaeta. The source of these rumors is easy to explain. Confused and terrified at the bestial cruelty of Commodus, the Romans refused to believe that the monarch-gladiator could have been the son of the emperor-philosopher. The man who, forgetting his dignity and his duties, amused himself with the retiarii [12] and took his part in fights in the arena could not be the son of the great Marcus Aurelius. He could, however, and his preferences seemed to confirm it, be the offspring of the empress's squalid relations with some unknown gladiator.

12. *Retiarii* were gladiators armed with a trident and a heavy net in which they sought to catch their opponents. Usually the *murmillones,* armed with a helmet, shield and sword, fought against them. It was among the latter that Commodus liked to fight during his extemporaneous gladiatorial exhibitions. In this context, see also note 14.

At the distance of eighteen centuries it is clear we can never know to what degree such stories are true. But in the face of the inextricable tangle of truth and distortion that the Roman literary sources have given us, the modern historian must, on many occasions, admit his defeat. And, withal, as in so many dime novels, there is too much sex, blood, and poison.

If Faustina had been a woman of no morals, we would never know it. We do know that she gave her husband many children and followed him often on his military campaigns. We do know that her husband, who was a sensitive and intelligent man, loved her tenderly in life and honored her greatly in death. In the *Recollections* in which Marcus Aurelius most often reveals the intimate details of his family life, the emperor defines his wife as obedient, loving, and without affectation. And the references to Faustina and the children which Fronto, writing to Marcus Aurelius, mixes with comments on his own poor state of health are those of a man who writes to a friend whose family life is serene and fortunate.

Halala, the remote town where Faustina died, took, on the wish of Marcus himself, the name of Faustinopolis and became a Roman colony. In this Asiatic village, as at Rome, temples were erected in honor of the dead empress whose assumption had placed her in the heaven of the gods. And Marcus, like Antoninus, never married again.

Though there is fathomless mystery in her life, numerous portraits on the coins of the period exist to speak about Faustina the Younger. We shall describe yet another. When this aureus bearing her portrait was struck, Faustina was already more than thirty years old. She was no longer the petted daughter of an old emperor but the wife of a young princeps busy defending his menaced state. But the head illustrated in Plate XXXI is the same that we have already encountered in the portraits of her early youth, alive, happy, and full of *joie de vivre.* The hair, the color of which is unfortunately not recorded by the gold but which must have been beautiful to have justified such attention, appears here waved and raised on the temples in a hairstyle *coup de vent* which would have pleased an Alexandre or an Antoine. It is a sure sign that even among plague [13] and invasion this ebullient young "Mater Castrorum" did not forget to take her tireless and inventive *ornatrices* with her to the Danubian encampment.

13. The plague, brought to Italy in 166 by troops returning from the Parthian campaign, raged for twenty years, claiming hundreds of thousands of victims.

# Lucilla and Crispina: the Faithless Women of the "Roman Hercules".

On March 17th, A.D. 180, Marcus Aurelius died at Vienna. The same ironic fortune that had cut short the life of the elegant and refined Faustina in a remote and dirty Anatolian village now sought the death of this intellectual man who wished only peace and leisure for study. Far from Rome and Athens, in a camp on the borders between the civilized world and the barbarians, the Stoic philosopher died on the Danubian *limes* like a simple soldier. And his entire life from the time when, at forty, he had taken the reins of empire into his hands had been nothing but a continued convulsive battle against the enemies and the adversities that had beset his realm.

The inheritance that Marcus Aurelius left to the Roman state on his death was terrible indeed. For eighty-four years without interruption sterility or the absence of male heirs had forced the emperors to make a virtue of necessity and choose their successors on the basis of their true gifts and capacities for government. The system of adoption gratified the Senate because, at least theoretically, the principate was open to all its members. But, what counted more, it had demonstrated itself to be the best system by giving the Roman state an uninterrupted series of distinguished principes. But Marcus had a son, and in Marcus too paternal affection showed itself to be stronger than philosophic wisdom.

It is not our duty to analyze to what degree Commodus was the degenerate monster described by the literary sources. Certainly the brief and wild life of this man who reached the imperial station before his nineteenth birthday was a bloody and terrible incubus for the senatorial class, and his violent death, like that of Nero, plunged the empire into a tragic civil war.

The fates of three women are dramatically intertwined with that of Commodus. They were Lucilla, his sister, Crispina, his wife, and Marcia, his mistress. Only the first two, however, are recorded by coin portraits.

Among the many daughters of Marcus and Faustina, Annia Lucilla was without doubt the most notable personality. She was born in 148 and at sixteen married the coemperor, Lucius Verus. Hers had been an electrifying experience, but one of brief duration. Only five years later, Lucius Verus died, and for unknown reasons Marcus Aurelius immediately obliged the young widow to marry an aged senator.

Forced to live beside a sick man and one with no political ambitions, from that moment on Lucilla's life was all pungent remorse for the happy times in which, as wife of her father's colleague, she had been, after Faustina, the most prominent woman of the empire. When, in 180, the principate passed to Commodus, and the prestigious role of empress was assumed by his beautiful wife Crispina, the frustrated ambition of Lucilla was transformed into jealousy and jealousy into a consuming hatred of her brother and the young woman to whom she saw her old fortunes pass. This hatred, toward the end of 182, found a monstrous outlet in an attempted fratricide. In senatorial circles violently hostile to the new princeps, it was certainly not difficult for Marcus's daughter to find a moral alibi and a wide support. But the hesitation of the assassin was fatal to the plotters, and the reaction of Commodus was, as might be expected, rapid and bloody. Lucilla was exiled to Capri, where a short time after Commodus had her killed. Five or six years afterwards, on the same island, there was to arrive, also as an exile, the young woman who in her young beauty and prestigious position had, without knowing it, set off the tragic fratricidal struggle between the two children of Marcus. And, for Brutia Crispina, guilty of adultery, the same inexorable order of execution that some years before had sealed the death of her awe-inspiring sister-in-law was to come from Rome.

In the splendid gallery of iconography given by imperial coinage, portraits of these two Augustae are certainly not absent. The face of Lucilla (Plate XXXIII) appears on an aureus coined when her father was still reigning. The face is a little fat and common but, nonetheless, in the features of the daughter of the philosopher-emperor one captures a slight reflection of that vivacity of expression which characterizes the portraits of Faustina the Younger. There is no trace of the frustrated ambition or of the rebellious character of Lucilla. Even in the unmistakable facial realism of the portrait, the face of Marcus's daughter remains, from the point of view of the expression, completely closed to any and every psychological study.

Very different is the portrait of the woman whom she hated and envied so much, Crispina. The beautiful but faithless wife of the "Roman Hercules"[14] appears as a young woman of pure and sad beauty. In the aureus in Plate XXXIV, without question one of the most beautiful female portraits of Roman coinage, Crispina appears with all her fascination. The graceful neck of an adolescent is adorned with a thin strand of beads. Her hair is gathered, with simplicity and elegance, behind the nape of her neck. And the dreamy depth of her gaze gives the face of the young Augusta that tone of aristocratic spirituality and at the same time of hidden melancholy which up to now we have met only on a few coin portraits of Octavia[15] and Agrippina the Elder[16]. We find the same expression on the magnificent sestertius illustrated in Plate XXXV above. The neck bends slightly forward and Crispina's gaze seems to stray towards the mysterious distance. The light brings out the waves of her hair, descends along her graceful neck and loses itself in the folds of her robe. In the play of soft shadows, the delicate face of the empress seems suffused with a deep melancholy. And in her sad expression there is almost a forethought of the tragic destiny which in a few years was to drag down this young woman.

After the elimination of his wife, Commodus did not marry again. During the last bloody and convulsive years of his tyranny he kept as a mistress Marcia, the ex-concubine of Quadratus, one of the plotters of 182 whom Commodus had had executed.

There is no coin to show the features of Marcia, certainly more powerful than

14. Commodus was not only immeasurably fond of gladiatorial games but participated in them himself. On various occasions he had fought in the amphitheatre and often in the course of such indecorous exhibitions had killed wild beasts. It was the Senate itself which servilely approved what he did by giving him the title "Hercules Romanus". There is no doubt that the emperor was pleased, because he had himself portrayed on statues and coins with his head covered by a lion's pelt, an attribute typical of the official iconography of Hercules. One of the coins on which Commodus appears wearing the lion's skin is reproduced in Plate XXXV below.

15. See Plate II.

16. See Plate VIII.

many empresses but never Augusta. However, it was she who, on the night of December 31, 192, brought to fruition the undertaking in which Lucilla and the others had failed. Strangled by one of those athletes among whom he had always liked to live, Commodus died at only thirty-one years of age.

With him, once again, the attempt to found a hereditary dynasty was extinguished in blood.

# Chapter 6

# THE SEVERANS

## From the Temple of the Sun at Emesa to the Imperial Palace of Rome: the Awe-Inspiring Julias and their Daughters-in-Law.

The crisis which had developed dramatically during the bloody reign of Commodus exploded in all its violence after the death of the young tyrant. Once again, as in the eighteen months after the death of Nero, it was the armies who forced their candidates upon the empire.

Pertinax, the old *praefectus urbis,* whom the assassins of Commodus had elevated to the principate with promise of a large donative for the Praetorians[1], maintained his hold on the empire for only three months. The same praetorian guard who assassinated him auctioned off the empire, knocking it down to Didius Julianus, a wealthy and aged senator who for 30,000 sestertii bought himself two months of agonizing power and a terrible death. And while this old, ambitious but unsoldierlike emperor tried in vain to fortify Rome, the legions of Syria, of Britain, and of the Danubian region proclaimed their own generals emperors.

1. But when an inspection of the imperial treasury was made, the new emperor found a ludicrously small sum (25,000 denarii) and so was unable to pay. This was certainly one of the causes of his abrupt end.

The civil war, ferocious and pitiless like all internal struggles, was to last for years, and at its end an inflexible African general, Septimius Severus, imposed his rule. During the following eighteen years of his reign, the existing evils of the Roman state, economic crises, wars on the frontiers, and the power of the armies, continued to fester under the apparent efficiency of an iron military government. In 211, when the old emperor died, no one and nothing was in a position to halt these forces of disintegration, and the empire fell into the terrible crisis of the third century from which it was never to recover completely.

The first women whose features are preserved on the coins of the troubled period following the death of Commodus are Manlia Scantilla and Didia Clara, the wife and daughter respectively of the ephemeral and slightly pathetic emperor Didius Julianus. We shall not pause to discuss these two women at length. We only know that, proclaimed Augustae by the Senate at the same time as the election of Didius, they followed the ambitious senator with fear, reluctance and a sense of foreboding to the imperial palace where they were to live in fear and uncertainty for only sixty days. Deprived of their titles and wealth by the triumphant Septimius Severus, there remained nothing for these guiltless victims of the ambition of an older man but to bury Didius and silently to melt into the shadows. Only the coins struck during the brief adventure of their husband and father remain today to testify to their ephemeral and involuntary moment of celebrity (Plates XXXVI and XXXVII).

A far different importance and personality belonged to the woman who entered the blood-stained palace on the Palatine after them. Julia Domna, for that was her name, was not only the cultivated and influential wife of Septimius Severus and later the watchful and sinister *éminence grise* of her son

Caracalla, but the foundress of a dynasty of awe-inspiring women, all of the same family, who, entering the palace through the marriage of Julia Domna, dominated the empire with varying fortunes up to the fall of the last of the Severi in 235. Beside Julia Domna, they were her sister, Julia Maesa, and Julia Maesa's two daughters, Julia Soaemias and Julia Mamaea. Their life was a bloody drama in which the most instinctive family affections were sacrificed to a delirium of ambition. And their death, with a single exception, was worthy of their life.

Septimius Severus, an African and a man of his age, was extraordinarily superstitious. The spiritual uneasiness of a tired civilization, the ever more common attraction toward the unknown in a world no longer satisfied by the classical religion, propelled more souls every day towards that obscure and magic universe which found its most elevated expression in the mystery religions of the Eastern provinces of the empire and its most fatal manifestations in magic, horoscopes and fortune-telling. It was on the basis of a horoscope that, in 185, the man of Leptis Magna, at the time a mere legate in Gallia Lugdunensis[2], picked his second wife. "Having learned that there was a girl in Syria, a certain Julia, whose horoscope destined her to become the wife of a king, he asked for her hand in marriage and, thanks to the help of friends, succeeded in marrying her. Shortly thereafter, he became a father"[3].

Thus did Julia Domna, daughter of Bassianus, priest of the Sun in the great temple at Emesa[4], become the wife of the thirty-nine-year-old African general, and after eight years of life in various provinces the prophecy of the stars came true and the young Syrian was raised to the rank of Augusta.

Among the Roman empresses there is no doubt that Julia Domna is one of the greatest and most tragic. Wherever the figure of Septimius Severus appears, in historical accounts, in inscriptions, in reliefs[5], in paintings[6], the ever-present image of the Syrian woman shadowing him shows the profound influence that this woman had on her imperial husband. On coins, too, there appears not infrequently the face of the Augusta behind the bearded head of Septimius. Let us look, for example, at the splendid aureus illustrated in Plate XXXVIII. While the head of the warrior-emperor is proudly set, his penetrating gaze straight ahead, a high radiate crown on his forehead, in a portrait calculated to bring together the elements of regal majesty, the face of the empress in the rear plane is inclined slightly in an attitude of troubled reflection. One might say that the artist wished to transfer to the coin portraits the profound psychological contrast between the intelligent but inflexible and energetic military man and the woman of Emesa deeply imbued with Greek culture, philosophy, and Oriental mysticism. The inscription, CONCORDIAE AETERNAE, which encircles this thought-provoking image, is not a hypocritical piece of propaganda because as long as Septimius lived, harmony did indeed unite the diverse natures of the superstitious African general and the refined Syrian intellectual. It was a harmony fed by the hopes of the new emperor and Julia. Indeed, even before the astrological predictions came true, in 186 and in 189, two children were born to the future emperor and his wife. Having conquered the imperial position, Septimius and Julia, without thought of the tragic experiences of the past, once more attempted to plant a hereditary monarchy on the suffering

2. Part of Gaul between the Loire, the Seine, the Marne and the Saône.

3. *Historia Augusta,* Life of Septimius Severus, 3.

4. Emesa, today Homs in Syria, was famous for the cult of the solar god Elagabal. In the temple of this divinity, whom the Romans worshipped as Invictus Sol Elagabalus, there was preserved and venerated a conical black stone that was believed to have fallen from heaven. The position of priest had been hereditary for centuries.

5. As, for example, in that of Leptis, or in that of Sievernich, or in that of the arch of the Argentarii at Rome.

6. As, for example, in the painting of Egyptian provenance today in Berlin.

body of the state. This hope was not only kept in their hearts but from the beginning of the reign it was part of the political program of the imperial couple. This is shown clearly by another splendid aureus struck in the very first years of the reign of Septimius Severus. Pescennius Niger and Clodius Albinus, the other pretenders to the throne of the unfortunate Didius Julianus, were still in arms in the East and in the West. But already in the portraits of little Caracalla and Geta, which face each other on the gold coin illustrated in Plate XXXIX, the program of imperial succession is set forth with the brief clarity of a modern propagandistic message.

The brief, laconic inscription, AETERNIT(ate) IMPERI(i), broadcasts the principle of dynastic continuity with the compression of a modern slogan. But if the reverse just described shows us once again that the propagandistic and informative function of Roman imperial coins made them much more than a simple means of exchange, even more interesting for our iconographic studies is the obverse of this exceptional coin. Julia Domna appears young and beautiful as she must have been in those first years of power. Her face has not yet suffered the devastating assault of time and tragedy. Quite the contrary, in the smooth and firm line of her forehead, in her great dreaming eyes, her firm and fair mouth, there is something of ingenuousness and purity which perplexes one if he thinks of the indomitable character already hidden behind this face. The hairdressing of the young Augusta is that in vogue at the end of the second century, the same which, in less elaborate form, we have already met on the coin portraits of the unfortunate ladies of the family of Didius Julianus. Parted at the top of the head, the locks descend in two large bands waved along the sides of the face to Julia's neck. They are then brought up behind the head and bound into an elaborate chignon which, by intricate braiding, makes a complicated pattern. One might say that after the ordered elegance of the hairstyles of Faustina the Younger, Lucilla and Crispina at the end of the century, taste returns to heavy and artificial hairstyles and, to judge from the truly astounding mass of hair, to the abundant use of falls and wigs.

Very different, not only in hairstyle, is the Julia Domna shown on the coin of Plate XL. Years have passed. Bitter experiences followed by a terrible family tragedy have worn out the youthful beauty of the Augusta but not her wild determination to dominate. The first battle was with a close counsellor of her husband's, Gaius Fulvius Plautianus, praetorian prefect, an African like Septimius and influential with him. The duel between the wife and friend of the emperor who were struggling for the first place in the heart of the princeps and for the power that automatically derived therefrom was carried on by every means. Plautianus's star reached its apex in 202, when the powerful praetorian prefect succeeded in having his young daughter, Plautilla, married to the sixteen-year-old Caracalla, the emperor's eldest son.

This was perhaps the most bitter moment for the ambitious Augusta. But her defeat was only apparent. She pretended to retire from the political battle to the wide circle of her eastern friends, to talk only of philosophy, history, religion. These are the years of her literary salon in which the cultivated empress anticipated by fourteen centuries Christina of Sweden and Madame de Sévigné. But Julia the philosopher, as Philostratus called her, was surely not so detached from terrestrial ambitions as to forget her enemy and the intrusion he had made in her family. Probably at the instigation of his mother, hatred in the soul of the young Caracalla against Plautilla and Plautianus grew day by day, and day by day the net of Julia Domna drew tight around her enemy. On January 22, A.D. 205, Plautianus, exposed for treason[7], fell in his own blood before Septimius and Caracalla in a room of the palace, and Plautilla, dragged down in her father's ruin, was exiled to Lipari. Julia Domna, now without a rival, began again to exercise her influence over the spirit of her husband and son.

7. Plautianus had been accused of treason by the dying Publius Septimius Geta, brother of Septimius Severus.

We have a moving portrait of the unfortunate Plautilla, innocent victim of this sordid struggle of ambition, on a denarius coined during the few years of her unhappy marriage (Plate XLII). The woman who, according to Dio Cassius, had brought to her husband a dowry "worthy of the marriage of fifty queens", the daughter of the powerful and feared praetorian prefect, appears as a fragile, almost adolescent girl. Even if we did not know her fate we could almost guess it from this slightly blurred portrait, suffused with a twilight melancholy. The face of the daughter of Plautianus is that of a serious and sad child, placed as a pawn in a game of powerful forces destined to destroy her. But this innocent creature was too dangerous for Julia Domna and her son to forget, even in exile on the distant island of Lipari. Six long years passed before the last protective shield against the implacable hatred of her sometime husband fell. In 211 this shield, Septimius Severus, fell and among the first victims of the bestial ferocity of Caracalla (Plate XLIII) was Plautilla, overtaken by a warrant for her death in that remote island.

After the drama of Plautianus, Severus's last six years rushed by in a murky accumulation of obscure omens. The warlike strength of the old princeps could still turn back the external enemies of the empire, but it was of no avail against the hatred which divided his two sons. Caracalla and Geta, the hope of the dynasty, the two children we have seen facing each other on the splendid aureus of Plate XXXIX, were now two men whom a thirst for power within their grasp drove inexorably against one another. On February 4, 211, at York in Britain, Septimius Severus ended his active life on earth. Gathered around the old general were Julia Domna and their two sons, the entire family, that is, whom the emperor had ordered to come to the front in the vain hope of arresting the spread of hatred between the brothers in the hard atmosphere of a military campaign. His last words were a prayer for harmony, good sense, and brotherly peace between the heirs to the empire. And then the end.

The last long voyage of the dead emperor to his capital across the sea, across Gaul and Italy, and the tragic events which, with an ever-increasing rhythm, followed one another at Rome, resemble the murky drama of a saga from the Nibelungenlied. Geta and Caracalla divided the imperial palace in two. They walled up the doors and the windows from one part to the other and settled in on the Palatine surrounded by their guards. For twelve months a menacingly somber quiet spread over Rome, and then the situation came to a head. One year after the death of Septimius Severus, Caracalla proposed a meeting of conciliation with his brother, and as neutral territory they chose Julia's apartment[8]. But suddenly from their hiding place appeared Caracalla's men. They

8. A few months before, the emperor's mother had firmly opposed a plan of separation of the empire between the two heirs of Septimius Severus. The proposal made by several of the counsellors was to assign the West to Caracalla and the East to Geta, in order to overcome the absurd situation that had been created and which, among other things, was grievously obstructing the administration of the state. Thus immediate urgency inspired a project which anticipated by a century and a half the division of the empire between Arcadius and Honorius.

assaulted Geta and stabbed him in the arms of his mother and in the presence of his brother.

Geta's blood, according to the ancient authors, stained the robes of Julia Domna, an unforgettable trauma that might have killed any ordinary woman. Mourn the lost son, fear the sight of the surviving brother, close oneself up and disappear forever: that is what it would be logical to expect a human being who had suffered such a great tragedy to do. But to withdraw and lament the ruin of one's own family meant withdrawing from public life, renouncing forever prestige, panoply, and circumstance savored during a reign of eighteen years. And it would mean renouncing ascendancy over a son who had already shown himself so subject to influence as to repudiate and exile his young wife. In a word, it meant giving up power, and a power that would be stronger now that there was no longer on the throne a man of the temper of Septimius Severus. Julia the philosopher knew all this and her aberrant ambition was stronger than maternal instinct. The years that followed saw the cynical choice of the Augusta solidified into a cordial participation in the government of the fratricide. Julia Domna followed Caracalla in his expeditions, gave him counsel, guided him, and had from her monstrous son that full power which Septimius had always rationed. Caracalla arrived at the throne when he was twenty-five. He had been divorced at nineteen but never married again or even took a concubine. The pathological ascendancy of Julia Domna over her son had no room for any other woman.

In the character of Caracalla and his mother we find for the first time the amazing consistency of the race of Bassianus, the consistency that we shall find again in all of the emperors and all of the women of this house: weak men, often perverted and cruel, always dominated by their mothers, and intelligent women, virilely decisive, thirsty for power, and ready to commit any crime to obtain it.

The coin in Plate XL, struck during the reign of Caracalla, shows a Julia Domna very different from the beautiful and sweet young woman shown on the aureus of twenty years before. Hardened by the years, made almost rapacious by the struggles around her, by her inner conflicts and by the ceaseless exercise of power, the face of the Augusta appears shut up in her heavy hairdressing as in a medieval helmet. In these years we find her most pretentious titles, "Mater Augusti Nostri et Castrorum et Senatus et Patriae"[9]. We well know what a bloody price had been paid for such maternal honors. But how tragically ironic, in turn, a simple coin legend can be is shown by this sestertius as well which has the legend IULIA PIA FELIX AUG[10] surrounding the worn and willful face of the mother of Geta. Pious and fortunate, then; it would be rather difficult to find in the dictionary two adjectives less suited to the nature and the life of this empress.

9. Mother of our Emperor, of the Soldiers, of the Senate and the Fatherland.

10. Julia, pious fortunate Augusta.

Let us turn over the coin and on the reverse we find a banal figure of Vesta seated on her throne (Plate XLI). Tired and inaccurate work of a mediocre engraver, the figure of the goddess is certainly not by the same hand that realized the magnificent head of Julia on the obverse. In the generic symbolism of the subject and in the poverty of its execution, the reverse of this sestertius shows us once again how the artistic genius of the Roman engravers of the imperial period was displayed above all in portraiture.

Caracalla's bloody reign was not long. In April, A.D. 217, during a campaign against the Parthians, the thirty-two-year-old sovereign was assassinated by a group of conspirators. There ascended to the throne at Rome Macrinus, praetorian prefect of the dead emperor and the guiding spirit of the conspiracy. The news reached Julia Domna at Antioch. After twenty-four years at the pinnacle of the state she could not resign herself to descending into the shadows. The world was full of inscriptions which proclaimed her glory in the past, and her face was carried by millions of coins that jingled in millions of purses. She had been glorified, great and powerful; how could she now return to being something else? Like Cleopatra, Julia Domna did not fear death, but mediocrity. And, like Cleopatra, she preferred suicide to facing a new state of things.

The assassination of Caracalla and the suicide of Julia Domna seemed to bring an era to a close. The family of Septimius Severus was destroyed, and no one of his race survived. So it seemed to everyone, and naturally to Macrinus among them. They underestimated one small fact: the dead empress had left her younger sister, Julia Maesa.

Julia Maesa had come court years before in the wake of her fortunate sister. By her husband, dead for many years, she had two daughters, Julia Soaemias and Julia Mamaea, and each of her daughters had given her a grandson. At the time of the death of Caracalla, these two women were living at Emesa with their widowed mother. Soaemias's son, Varius Avitus, whom history has called Elagabalus after his god, was not yet fourteen. Every day in the temple at Emesa this strangely fascinating boy worshipped with mystical ecstasy that solar divinity whose priesthood he held, like his great-grandfather so many years before, as an hereditary right. His cousin, Julia Mamaea's son, was nine years old and was named Gessius Bassianus. A few years later the world was to know him by his imperial name Alexander Severus.

Relegated by Macrinus to Emesa, Julia Maesa must have felt a deep nostalgia for the happy years passed in the far-off capital. The brilliant life of Rome, the splendid salons of the imperial palace, the power which her sister reflected upon her seemed, amid the restricted horizons of Emesa, to be a source of joy that the aging woman could not give up. A firm determination to reconquer this lost paradise drove Maesa, and with her all the clan of the Bassiani, to dare the impossible before the power of Macrinus could be consolidated.

The third legion Gallica, one of the large units that a few months before Caracalla was to have led against the Parthians, was still camped at Raphaneae, a few miles from Emesa. While Macrinus did nothing, thoughts of the military undertakings, of the generous donatives of Septimius and of Caracalla ran through the minds of the soldiers and officers and became magnified. Julia Maesa understood that it was necessary to offer these troops two things: much, yes, very much money, and a noble cause. The money was at hand; the noble cause was not, but it was quickly invented. Varius Avitus, the fourteen-year-old priest of the Sun, suddenly ceased to be the son of a worthy but socially unimportant father, now fortunately deceased, and assumed the role of the illegitimate son of Caracalla. The mother of the young man, Julia Soaemias, had no objection to this transformation but was proud to confirm the fact. The boy was brought at night to the camp of the third legion Gallica and was acclaimed by the soldiers, who were almost all Syrians. The troops were ready to fight to place the young son of their assassinated emperor on the usurped throne.

To Macrinus, tarrying at Antioch, the affair appeared at first glance to be a joke, but it was hardly a joke to see sent back the head of his prefect Julianus whom he had sent to nearby Emesa to bring back the head of the boy. Nor was there any joking shortly afterwards in the battle between Maesa's army and his own. Maesa and Soaemias got out of their litters and threw themselves like Furies between the combatants to urge on their own. And under the eyes of these two awe-inspiring women even the young Elagabalus fought with inspired fury for the first and last time in his brief life.

It was June 8, A.D. 218. With Macrinus put to flight and then murdered, the avenue of return to the so much desired capital was opened up before Maesa and her daughters. With them travelled Elagabalus and his small cousin, the indispensable instruments of their future power.

Elagabalus was not sparing of gratitude towards the women who had devised his triumph. Among the first honors given to his grandmother and mother was, naturally, the title Augusta and the right to be portrayed on coins. Thus among the hands of the subjects of the great empire the features of the fateful women of Emesa reappeared on gold, silver and bronze. Let us also look at them ourselves. Julia Maesa, the principal architect of this success, appears on a sestertius illustrated in Plate XLIV as a woman already old. On this face marked by time and her adventures, we look in vain for a trace of the facial beauty of the latest coin portraits of her great sister[11]. The facial traits of the true mistress of the empire seem extremely hard, almost masculine. Even her hairdressing seems to be simplified in order not to clash with her hard, cold virago face.

11. See Plate XL.

Very different is the appearance of the elder of her two daughters, Soaemias, on a denarius illustrated in Plate XLV. Hers is also an unattractive face, but in its look and expression there is not the dominating force of Maesa. We know that Julia Soaemias, when she arrived at Rome, led a life of shameful excesses. Drunk with power, the woman who had thrown herself into the mêlée of the decisive battle like a soldier could not maintain the cold detachment of her mother but allowed herself to be drawn into that vortex of depravity which ended by dragging her down together with her son. It is, therefore, the lascivious impression of an intemperate life that the unknown engraver of this coin succeeds in giving to the still-youthful features of Maesa's daughter. In the great bulb of the eye barely projecting below heavy eyebrows, in the swollen and prominent lower lip and in the pursing of the mouth, we see something flaccid, the traits of an illness of sensuality. As in a mirror, the face of Soaemias reflects the pathological degeneration also visible in the face of her son Elagabalus (Plate XLV below).

The heads of the women whom the young priest of the Sun had struck in coin portraits during his brief reign were not only those of his grandmother and

12. Elagabalus with his suite arrived at Rome only in the first days of July A.D. 219, over a year after his final victory over Macrinus.

mother. In the less than three years between his arrival at Rome and his death [12] Elagabalus had married and repudiated three wives. The first was Julia Paula. He married her in A.D. 219 and repudiated her a year later, depriving her, naturally, of the title of Augusta as well. Then there was the turn of a Vestal, Aquilia Severa. Elagabalus seduced her and married her, perfectly disdainful of the scandal that a sacrilege of the sort aroused among the Romans. From his strange point of view, however, a marriage between him, a great priest of the Sun, and a priestess of Vesta appeared almost a holy union between the superior religion of his Oriental god and the more traditional and autochthonous religion of the Italian cults, almost a duplication, with living beings, of the sacred marriage celebrated by him a short time before between the image of his god and the Carthaginian heavenly Juno whose statue had been brought for the purpose to Rome. However, Aquilia Severa also must have quickly bored the unbalanced emperor. In 221 it was another young woman who received, together with the ephemeral role of wife, the title Augusta. She was Annia Faustina. But after a few months Annia Faustina was also repudiated and banished from the palace, leaving her place and title to Aquilia Severa who thus returned unexpectedly into the good graces of the fickle emperor.

Names and portraits are all that we have to recall these three women, speeding meteorites without any importance in the eventful history of those years. But in their young faces we can still find a distant reflection of their diverse characters and different aspirations. The face of Julia Paula on a denarius shown in Plate XLVI is the young face of a girl who has not yet left the dreams of adolescence to enter fully on adult life. The face of Aquilia Severa, the Vestal Virgin, is also young, but more experienced, less trusting, as if covered by a shadow of melancholy. We do not know if her sacrilegious marriage was an act of free choice dictated by ambition or a rape by a paranoid monster. It is certain, however, that it was the cause of interior conflicts which seem to appear in the caremarked face of Aquilia which has come down to us on the very fine sestertius illustrated in Plate XLVII above.

We find neither sadness nor joy in the expression of Annia Faustina, the third wife of Elagabalus (Plate XLVII below). She had been widowed only a short time when the emperor proposed marriage. Of her, probably the eldest of the three, we have the most neutral and colorless portrait. Beneath her swelling forehead, her large, inexpressive eyes tell us nothing of her character, her ambitions, or her illusions. Her face is not one of those that one remembers.

In A.D. 221, in the very year in which Annia Faustina was living her ephemeral imperial adventure, another woman of far different stature as a politician was rapidly solidifying the prodigious work carried out a few years before. Julia Maesa, the awe-inspiring old woman, architect of the fortunes of Elagabalus, had understood for some time that the army, the Senate, and the people of the capital would not tolerate for long the exotic mysticism, the unspeakable perversions and the total incapacity for government shown by her grandson. Soon, very soon, some unknown general would be elevated as emperor in some far-off province. That would be the end, not only for Elagabalus, but for all the race of the priests of Emesa. But to maintain her hold on the dizzy pinnacle she had attained with such good fortune, it was necessary once again to anticipate events. The possibility of a crime that would pull down one of her daughters and her grandson by her own wish did not deter her. But there was at court the other daughter, Julia Mamaea, and her son, the thirteen-year-old Gessius Bassianus, who seemed, young as he was, to be the very opposite of Elagabalus. This would be the new candidate for emperor before others foreign to the family clan of Emesa might spontaneously appear.

Julia Maesa's maneuver was simple and diabolical at the same time. Once again her vast means served to buy the support of the praetorians for her young grandson. Once again, spread by Maesa's wiles and confirmed by Mamaea, rumors were circulated that the thirteen-year-old Bassianus was also a bastard son of Caracalla. By July 10, 221 the first phase of the plot was complete. Elagabalus was persuaded by Maesa to associate himself with a colleague who would save him from the troubles and inconveniences of governing and permit him to dedicate himself even more completely to the adoration of his god. And so, Elagabalus, at seventeen, agreed to adopt his thirteen-year-old cousin. The second act of the operation took care of itself as Maesa had foreseen. On March 11, A.D. 222, Elagabalus and his mother Soaemias were slaughtered and thrown into the Tiber by the praetorians who proclaimed Gessius Bassianus, not yet fourteen years old, emperor with the name Alexander Severus. No sign of remorse or of hesitation disturbed Maesa's cold lucidity when she sacrificed a daughter and a grandson on the altar of the dynasty. Julia Mamaea was not inferior to her.

As could be foreseen, Maesa undertook to establish the new order and turn Alexander Severus's nascent empire into new paths. With an iron hand, the imperial palace was cleansed of that colorful collection of homosexuals, intriguing freedmen, effeminates and dubious servants who had invaded it during the reign of Elagabalus. The state was brought back to Roman traditions, and valuable men like Ulpian were called to the government. Julia Mamaea and Severus were once again the docile instruments of the will of Julia Maesa who governed the destiny of the Roman state for four years with singular ability and a virile hand.

In 226, death overtook the aged princess who for more than thirty years had been a witness and protagonist of so many bloody events. The most ferocious of the four Julias of Emesa was the only one to die in peace in her bed.

The sole survivor of the group, Julia Mamaea, remained now together with her son who had reached seventeen years of age. Alexander Severus was certainly not Elagabalus. And yet, from infancy he had become accustomed to obey exceptionally authoritarian and energetic women, and his whole life had been dominated by his mother. In 225 he had married Orbiana, but Julia Mamaea, as in the past Julia Domna, was not a woman to tolerate a female presence that was not her own beside her son. It required a couple of years to undermine the marriage. In 227, Orbiana was repudiated and exiled to Africa. There remains a soft portrait of her on a rare sestertius coined during the brief period of her good fortune (Plate XLIX)[13], while an interesting medallion in bronze (Plate XLVIII) preserves a rather unusual image of her awe-inspiring mother-in-law. Julia Mamaea appears in a full-bust portrait in which the desire to make a regal

13. On the reverse of this coin (see the Descriptive Index of Coins on page 120) Orbiana and Alexander Severus are shown standing in the act of shaking hands. The representation and the legend CONCORDIA AUGUSTORUM which surrounds it lead one to think that this sestertius was coined in 225 to celebrate the wedding of the young emperor.

and supernatural effect is not sufficient to hide the limitations of the engraver. The mother of the emperor appears in the guise of a winged divinity, her head bound with a diadem ornamented at its peak by a lotus flower, her right arm bent to hold a heavily burdened cornucopia, her left hand raised and holding a burning torch ornamented with grain ears. From her heavy robe there emerges a long, thin neck *à la Boldini,* behind which there appears a crescent moon. The face, in spite of the aristocratic features and the detached expression, keeps the facial features of Mamaea clearly marked, with no concession to idealization [14]. This unusual representation of the Augusta offers the observer an impression of almost superhuman majesty, more in Oriental than in Roman taste. Certainly the limitations of the author of this ambitious portrait cannot escape a sharp eye. The hands, always very difficult to represent, are approximately rendered but inordinately large and thus out of proportion to the face and the chest of the Augusta. The drapery, which is used in vain as a device to hide the insuperable difficulties in perspective of a three-quarters bust encountered by the engraver, appears, all in all, as a confused pastiche. But in spite of all this, none of the coin portraits of Julia Mamaea gives us such a thought-provoking image of the mother of the emperor. And above all, no other portrait radiates that sense of inspired, almost mystical regality which we find in this medallion and which so effectively symbolizes the immutable will to power, not only of Mamaea but of all this race of women come from the east to change the history of Rome.

Julia Mamaea had the same ambition and the same thirst for power as Domna and Maesa. She did not, however, have the alert intelligence of her aunt or the cold determination of her mother. Through her insatiable thirst for money, her favoritism and the continual imposition of her will on her client-son, she lost in the end.

On March 18, A.D. 235, in the military camp of Mainz, a gang of mutineers killed her together with the twenty-five-year-old emperor. With Alexander Severus and Julia Mamaea the dynasty of Emesa was extinguished forever.

14. The unknown author of the coin has thus gathered in this interesting image of Mamaea the attributes of five divinities: Victory (the wings), Isis (the lotus flower), Diana (the crescent moon), Abundantia (the cornucopia), and Ceres (the torch adorned with grain). A representation of this sort clearly shows the strong syncretic tendencies of the religion of the time.

Chapter 7

# MILITARY ANARCHY

## The Short-Reigned Lords of War and their Ladies.

1. March 18, A.D. 235.

2. November 17, A.D. 284.

3. While Alexander Severus was reigning at Rome, civil war in Persia brought to power Ardashir, a noble who claimed descent from the Achaemenid dynasty defeated five hundred years before by Alexander the Great. With Ardashir (Artaxerxes I) the Sassanian dynasty was founded. It was to endure until the Islamic conquest.

The period of exactly fifty years which separates the assassination of Alexander Severus[1] and the elevation of Diocletian[2] to the throne of the empire was the most tragic and chaotic in the long history of Rome.
In the east, the new Sassanian dynasty[3] brought to the old Persian state an expansive vigor which pinned down Roman armies in a continual and debilitating struggle. On the long fortified line which marked the northern boundaries of the empire along the Rhine and the Danube, ever-greater masses of barbarians appeared, like an irresistible avalanche. And while across the ruptured German *limes* the savage hordes of Goths, Alemanni and Franks spread out over all the provinces of the empire, the plague once again ravaged and worked havoc among the tormented population.
Beneath the blows of such reverses, the Roman state seemed on the point of final collapse. The growing disasters of invasion and epidemic were augmented by the scourge of two old ills that had long been incubated in the body of the empire and had dramatically matured during the unfortunate period of the women of Emesa: the disastrous economic crisis and the power of the military. Thus, in the collapse of the entire economic system the old silver denarius was rapidly devalued and left the field to an unordered mass of valueless coins and the legions, knowing full well that they were the only force capable of resuscitating the empire, placed on the throne in turn their most prominent commanders. In the brief span of these terrible fifty years, fully forty men tasted, some for only a few days, the bitter and intoxicating potion of supreme power.
For the most part, we do not have portraits of the women of these ephemeral warlords. Others are often known only by their portraits, and are shadowy figures who in general did not have the time to reveal their personality, strong or insignificant as it might be. They were elevated to the role of Augusta after years of tiring peregrinations with their soldier-husbands among the obscure garrisons of the provinces. Many held the position to which they were elevated for no more than a few months or at most for a year or so. This was the destiny of Paulina, of Otacilia Severa, of Cornelia Supera (Plates L, LII, LIII below), wives respectively of Maximinus Thrax, of Philip the Arab, and of Aemilianus. The fate of others of these women was different. For example, the wife of Gordian III, Tranquillina (Plate LI) was married to the youthful emperor by her father, the able and scheming praetorian prefect Timesitheus, who by means of his daughter's marriage aimed not only at satisfying his own ambition but also and above all at reinforcing his own great power.
Others of these women died before their husbands reached power or, by a bitter turn of fate, soon after their elevation to the throne. This was almost certainly the fate of Paulina and Mariniana, the wives of Maximinus Thrax and

Valerian. Given the silence of ancient sources concerning them, it is the coins struck in their names which narrate their history. The heads of these two Augustae, indeed, are always veiled and their names are preceded by the adjective "Diva" on all their coins, showing clearly that both Paulina and Mariniana were already dead and deified when the first coin issues in their honor were ordered (Plates L above and LIV). The peacock, as well, which invariably appears on the reverse of their coins accompanied by the legend CONSECRATIO (Plate L below) makes allusion to the consecration of Paulina and Mariniana in the heavens of the immortals because of the role of the peacock as the sacred bird of Juno.

There remain portraits, with uncovered heads, of Tranquillina, already mentioned above, of Cornelia Supera, wife of Aemilianus, and of Etruscilla, the wife of Trajan Decius (Plate LIII above). On a series of antoniniani, coins of which the inferior manufacture and poor metal content show the profound misery of the period, the faces of these Augustae have no message for us. They are figures that materialize in simple outline in an age of iron. The only detail over which the hasty hand of the engraver seems to pause is perhaps the complex hairstyle and robe of the period. The hair may be closely waved with the help of a heated iron, or fall free in its natural wave, coming down behind the ears to the nape of the neck and then, gathered and bound in a large soft braid, is brought up again to the top of the head. This is certainly the commonest of the elegant hairstyles of the third century. It is found again in almost the same form in the portrait of Magnia Urbica, wife of Carinus, whose features, the only record of her existence, are preserved on a very rare aureus illustrated in Plate LVII. That the hairstyle of Tranquillina, Cornelia Supera, Etruscilla and Magnia Urbica was not the only one in vogue among women of high Roman society of this period is shown by an interesting coin portrait of Severina, wife of Aurelian, during whose brief meteoric reign a united empire seemed to raise itself up again against all its former enemies[4]. This Augusta, whose name alone is known to history, appears as a mature woman with a hard, marked face and a furrowed brow. Her hair is combed back over the temples to the nape of the neck and then, without being gathered in a braid or a chignon, is bent back in a simple, wide curve that winds around her head and ends on the forehead in a soft, large wave which, finally brought back again, is anchored on the crown of the head with a rich diadem. It is a quiet and at the same time elegant hairstyle which contrasts strangely with the sour face of the wife of Aurelian. The engraver of this antoninianus (Plate LVI) seems to play with this contrast, pausing over the detailed representation of this refined hairstyle and at the same time pitilessly portraying the deep furrows of the empress's forehead, her small and insignificant eye, her vulgar profile and bull-like neck[5].

Portraits of the other Augustae of the third century, in addition to the usual images appearing on antoniniani, are preserved on the interesting and especially valuable medallions of the period. These were coined in large numbers, perhaps for court dignitaries and perhaps for individuals retiring from the military or civil service. And the medallions of the middle years of the third century are often accurate and programmatic portraits of the imperial family.

4. Arriving at the emperorship no longer young but still vigorous, the Illyrian Aurelian succeeded during his brief reign (270-275) in reunifying the empire. With extraordinary energy he defeated the barbarians who menaced the north frontier and reduced them to obedience. Then he destroyed the power of Zenobia and recovered the eastern provinces that had fallen under the sway of the queen of Palmyra. Finally, he brought to an end the separatist movement in Gaul and reunited the so-called Imperium Galliarum to Rome.

5. Just as much as the obverse, the reverse of this piece (illustrated in the Descriptive Index of Coins on page 123) is of great interest. The type is a standing figure of Concordia holding two military standards. Around the type there runs the legend CONCORDIAE MILITUM (unity of the soldiers). A type like this, so unusual for the coin of an Augusta, leads one to suppose that this antoninianus was coined during the few weeks of the interregnum which followed the assassination of Aurelian in the autumn of 275. In these circumstances, the appeal for "the unity of the soldiers" of the coins of the widow of the warrior-emperor would have a precise and highly dramatic meaning.

The portrait of the emperor, of the Augusta, and of the heir to the throne appear together, while the legend CONCORDIA AUGUSTORUM which surrounds these idyllic family portraits reveals in words, together with the mute language of the representation, the desire, all too human for anyone who has reached supreme power, to transmit to his descendants what he has personally conquered by arms and often by treachery and assassination.

In this way the aspiration of Philip the Arab to install a dynasty of his blood on the throne is evident when one looks at the splendid bronze medallion in Plate LII. In an epoch in which the great Roman tradition of portraiture still gives us images of a strong verism, even on common coins, the author of this medallion, in a desire to produce not just a simple means of exchange but a prized object for an elite, a medallion whose only motivation was beauty, makes an admirable essay in the style of verism which, sinking its deepest roots in the great portrait tradition of the coins of the Hellenistic Ptolemies, Seleucids, and the other monarchs of the kingdoms born of the total disintegration of the kingdom of Alexander the Great, is the most continuous and important element in Roman coin art from the epoch of Augustus to the advent of Diocletian.

Without giving in to the temptation of court art to idealize Philip and his family, but also without seeking the easily-obtained effect of exaggeration, the engraver of this splendid die gives us psychological studies of exceptional power of three imperial individuals, and unites them in an image of rare aesthetic balance. The face of the Arab who bounded prodigiously from the desert of Trachonitis[6] to the throne of the Caesars is shown with rough force almost emblematic of the era. In the background, behind the rough but not cruel face of the soldier, there are the simple and tranquil features of Otacilia Severa, the wife who followed him first in his minor career as an officer and then in his meteoric rise. Lastly, placed before his parents, in a position emphasized by its isolation, M. Julius Severus Philippus, the hope of the empire, the future of the new dynasty for which the solemn celebrations of the first thousand years of Rome itself seemed to give a secure omen of good fortune[7]. When this medallion was struck, the son of Philip the Arab was probably ten years old. After the defeat and repulse of the Parthians and the Germans who had invaded the empire, Philip had raised his son to the rank of Augustus during the celebration of his triumph in A.D. 247. On the occasion of the thousandth anniversary of the state, therefore, fortune seemed to smile on the forty-three-year-old soldier, on his quiet wife, and on the sour-faced boy whose family expressions, in all their diversity, were captured in this bronze coin by an unknown engraver in a refined psychological counterpoint. But the iron forces of his time did not save Philip and his family from the destiny that he himself had served to his predecessor. In 249 the man who had conquered the throne by betraying and killing the young Gordian III was betrayed and killed by Decius, a successful general whom he himself had sent to fight the Germans. The young Philip also fell at the hands of the praetorians. Only concerning the fate of Otacilia Severa does history remain silent.

Another family portrait, similar but very different at the same time from that of the medallion of Philip the Arab, appears on a silver medallion of Gallienus illustrated in Plate LV. In this case, too, the exaltation of the family group

6. Today, Hawaran, a region on the borders of Syria and Iraq.

7. In A.D. 248.

shows an attempt to spread the idea of dynastic continuity. But what a difference there is between this die and that of the epoch of Philip!

The simple fact that the family of Gallienus is not portrayed on the same side of the medallion breaks the necessary unity of the representation. Indeed, while the opposed portraits of Gallienus and his wife Salonina occupy one side of the coin, on the other there appear busts of Valerian I and Valerian II, father and son respectively of the great emperor. In contrast to the animated and unmistakable face of the only emperor who succeeded in keeping his throne for over a decade in this troubled period, the anonymous face of Salonina appears to belong to an even less distinct personality than is in reality the case. There is no doubt that the two portraits were done with care and by a practiced hand. The engraver certainly knew that in the case of a die for a medallion his finished work would be scrutinized by the eye of the man of refined taste who governed his empire with a hand of iron. But the consummate portrait ability of the artist was not accompanied by the compositional taste of the master of the period of Philip the Arab.

The animated and asymmetrical depth in the portrait of the family of Philip the Arab, achieved by placing the images on different planes, and the open effect of the large empty space below the portraits of the three Augusti, has been replaced in the medallion of Gallienus by the pure and simple opposition of the bust of the emperor and his wife which mirror with tedious monotony the identical arrangement of the portraits of Valerian I and his grandson on the other side of the medallion [8]. This is the same composition that we have found on the aureus of Agrippina and the young Nero [9], a compositional scheme, therefore, of two hundred years before. Even the legend which, set out in a perfect semicircle, gives the medallion an almost architectural structure, as if it were a triumphal arch placed over the heads of the emperor and his family, becomes nothing other than a mere explicative description when placed in the lower part of the coin of Gallienus.

Thus, the case is the same for coins which were simple means of exchange and artistically refined medallions, imperial gifts destined for a few hands; the artistic sensibility of the engravers shows itself in a thousand almost imperceptible details which, gathered in the final synthesis of the work, set off a true artist from the able craftsman who may be the master of his trade but is completely deprived of inspiration.

8. Not illustrated on the plates. The reproduction of the two sides of this medallion may be found in the Descriptive Index of Coins on page 122.

9. See Plate XV.

Chapter 8

# THE TETRARCHS AND THE AGE OF CONSTANTINE

## Prisca and Valeria: the Family Tragedy of Diocletian.

The argument between the young officer and Dryas, the proprietor of a small inn in the territory of the Tungri [1], had become heated. In the country inn, this man, one of the many rough Illyrian soldiers who at this time were common in the scattered garrisons of the empire, had been enjoying himself. But, as he prepared to leave, the bill presented to him seemed exaggerated. And it was over this that he was arguing with the proprietress. When Dryas, half in jest but half-seriously, accused him of miserliness, the officer replied jokingly, "When I am emperor, then I'll be generous!" But the innkeeper answered, "Diocletian, don't joke; you shall be emperor for sure when you kill a wild boar!" [2]

It was fifteen years later, on November 17, A.D. 284, that the Roman troops on the Persian front discovered the emperor Numerian assassinated in his litter. Aper, the praetorian prefect and the brother-in-law of Numerian, the man whom everyone believed to be the assassin, was dragged before the stage erected in the center of the encampment. Before passing judgment on the prisoner, however, the troops wanted to acclaim the new emperor, C. Aurelius Valerius Diocletianus. The first public act of the newly-elected princeps was to kill Aper with his own sword [3]. In this way the prediction made so many years before by the Gallic innkeeper came true in a far-off camp in the east.

Diocletian was forty-six years old, of humble birth, and the product of the inexhaustible source of soldiers that Illyria had become at this time. Because of his origins and the manner of his acclamation, Diocletian seemed destined to pursue the same parabola as the ephemeral emperors who had preceded him. But from time long past when Dryas made her prediction, the Dalmatian officer had been able to study the two constant factors which had undermined the basis of rule of fully five emperors.

The same chain of events had brought down Aurelian, Tacitus, Probus, Carus, Numerian; however different these men might have been in character, intelligence and ability. Above all, it was clear that one man was not enough to shore up the immense and ramshackle edifice of the empire. A single emperor could only carry on a weakened and hopeless battle against the uninterrupted barbarian invasions which burst over the borders, against the continual revolutions of usurpers, and against the tenacious separatist movements of the provinces. And even when an exceptional personality such as Aurelian succeeded, by supreme effort, in unifying and welding together the collapsing empire, there was always the insidious danger of conspiracy against which intelligence, courage and strength were of no use. With nightmarish regularity, the five predecessors of Diocletian had died at the point of daggers or

1. The Tungri were a people of Gallia Belgica in the present-day territory of Liège.

2. The anecdote is recounted in the *Historia Augusta,* Life of Carus, Carinus and Aemilianus, 14.

3. After having dispatched Aper Diocletian cried "Finally I have killed the proper wild boar!" This is a play on words between the name of the praetorian prefect and the name of the animal (in Latin *aper* is wild boar).

through poison after only a few months or years of unhappy power. The brutal consequences of the violence adopted by the armies of the third century led to habitual regicide.

Experience and wisdom, therefore, led Diocletian to his immediate decision to divide supreme power with Maximian, a faithful companion in arms and an Illyrian like himself. Diocletian was to wage wars in the eastern part of the empire, Maximian in the west. The defense of the immense territory thus became possible, while a conspiracy capable of eliminating the two Augusti at the same time in their residences thousands of miles apart became a desperate enterprise.

After nine years of united government, Diocletian further perfected his system. Galerius and Constantius Chlorus, two excellent Illyrian officials, joined the Augusti as Caesars, that is to say as designated heirs of the empire. But that was not all. The iron will of Diocletian wished to consolidate the solidarity of the four princes by bonds of blood. Galerius had to repudiate his wife and marry Valeria, the daughter of Diocletian, while Theodora, the step-daughter of Maximian, married Constantius who, in turn, was forced to abandon his mistress, that Helena for whom destiny had reserved an unpredictably brilliant future.

We know little about Theodora. We have only an insignificant portrait of her issued posthumously on a small bronze coin of the period of the sons of Constantine (Plate LIX above).

Valeria, on the other hand, the daughter of Diocletian, had an adventurous and tragic life. After the voluntary retirement of her father in 305, she remained for six years at the side of Galerius, who had now become emperor. Hers was certainly not a happy marriage. Through that strange fate that unites so many royal couples of every period and place, no child came to warm the coldness of a political marriage. And as long as Galerius lived, Valeria, a Christian sympathizer and perhaps already a secret Christian in her heart, had to witness the last and most rabid persecution of the new and widespread religion conducted by her very own husband.

But if life had not been kind to this princess, her end was tragic indeed. When Galerius died in A.D. 311, Valeria retired with her mother Prisca to Maximinus Daia, nephew and adopted son of her husband. Diocletian's daughter was certainly intelligent enough to understand that the delicate system created by her father, once the coordinating genius of Diocletian was removed, could and did generate a monster of civil war. And while, in the east and west, Constantine, Maxentius, Licinius and Maximinus were eagerly gathering troops and money for the imminent struggle, Valeria was seeking only a bit of peace. But fate decreed that the widow of Galerius was not to find it. A proposal of marriage arrived from Maximinus who, in the coming crisis, would have made excellent use of her name and her wealth. But Valeria refused. The reaction of Maximinus Daia was that of a wild oriental despot and it extended to the entire small court of Valeria. It was in vain that the old Diocletian, who was living like a rich country gentleman, requested that permission be given to his wife and daughter to reach his palace at Spalato. Prisca and Valeria, after a travesty of a trial, were shamefully conducted through the streets of those provinces which for thirty years had acclaimed them as empresses. Then, after suffering every sort of abuse, they were exiled to a far-off Syrian village.

In the meantime, the struggle between Licinius and Maximinus spread with violence. In the general confusion, the two unfortunates succeeded in taking flight and, disguised as ordinary women, sought to reach Spalato. Their desperate wandering lasted for fifteen months, fifteen months of continual fright, sudden escapes, and fatiguing movement through the troubled provinces towards a goal which seemed unobtainable.

Their persecutor was dead. But in the palace of Nicomedia the victor Licinius seemed to surpass in ferocity even the human monster that he had annihilated shortly before. In some city of Asia, or in Greece, in a tavern or on the road, the two fugitives heard that Diocletian had died. They no longer had a goal. Finally, in a street of Salonika, someone recognized them and informed the soldiers. They were taken and beheaded in a square of the city. Then the bodies of the wife and the daughter of the great Diocletian were thrown into the sea.

No coin portrait of Prisca exists. But there is the portrait of Valeria on the follis[4] illustrated in Plate LVIII. Even if this coin betrays our hopes of knowing the real features of this unhappy princess, it marks, from a stylistic point of view, a fundamental development in coin iconography of imperial Roman women. If we observe the face of the unfortunate wife of Galerius, we realize that now, for the first time in three centuries, there is a coin portrait of an Augusta that is intended to be neither crudely veristic nor classically idealized. In this face we seek in vain the pure idealization of the portrait of Livia such as appears on the dupondius in Plate V. In vain we look for the animated though sometimes pitiless verism which in its highest forms reaches psychological portraiture of a rare power which is shown by the face of Octavia on the aureus of Plate II and on the head of Julia Domna on the sestertius of Plate XL, to give only two examples.

4. Between 295 and 296 Diocletian carried out a far-reaching monetary reform. At this time, new types of coins were instituted, among which was the follis of bronze.

Every remaining trace of the individual physiognomy of Valeria is cancelled by her squared head, taurine neck, and the geometric pattern of rigid vertical lines dominating the neck, forehead, nose and entire expression. This is the typical coin style of the period of the tetrarchs. It is a style which dominates the coinage, but is less frequent in the major arts and in sculpture is limited to a few images in porphyry among which may be included the mysterious and fascinating group of tetrarchs inserted in the corner between the Basilica of San Marco and the Doge's Palace in Venice[5].

5. Other sculptures of this type can be found respectively in the Vatican, at Niš, and in Istanbul. As stated above, all these works are carved in porphyry, the very hard red Egyptian stone reserved for imperial monuments.

The coin portraits of the emperors of this period appear hardly different from the portrait of Valeria. We may look, for example, at the face of Constantius Chlorus on the coin illustrated in Plate LIX below. Strong, simple lines make up the massive profile, the unrealistically bull-like neck, the prominent eye, the ear which is given a stylized almond shape, the simple outline of the hair and of the beard which is made in a compact mass gathered in small furrows by an engraving tool. Adherence to reality is lost, and consequently the sense of plasticity has also been lost. The features of Constantius Chlorus and Valeria are made into flat, stylized images in which graphic requirements prevail.

These are no longer portraits of individual sovereigns, but abstract and motionless images of royalty itself. It is here, in this moment and in these coins, that one recognizes the great change that brings an end to the art of antiquity and signifies the beginning of Byzantine and medieval culture. In the extremely massive and now completely stylized faces of the tetrarchs and of the daughter of Diocletian, art becomes infused with the spiritual restlessness of a world thirsting for transcendence, a world that has already turned its back on the old pagan anthropomorphic religion to plunge into the mystical mystery cults of Christ and Mithras.

A few years later, the triumph of Constantine was to mark the definitive victory of Christianity. And the new world, formed in the massive stylization of the tetrarchic image, would find the first monetary expression of royal Christianity in the abstract and refined linearity of certain coins of the sons of Constantine.

## Saint Helena: the Meteoric Rise of the Tavern-Girl of Niš.

When Constantius was raised by Diocletian to the prestigious role of Caesar, he was forced, as we have seen, to sacrifice the woman who had been the free choice of his heart to motives of state. Helena, the mistress whom he was forced to abandon to marry Theodora [6], was still a beautiful woman although no longer young [7]. Constantius, called Chlorus because of his pallid complexion, had made her acquaintance twenty years before in a tavern of Naissus [8], where Helena was employed in the none-too-respectable job of *stabularia.* She was therefore a tavern servant-girl, in the ancient world almost synonymous with prostitute [9]. In spite of these circumstances, the young Illyrian officer fell in love with her and took her with him. At some time, perhaps in A.D. 273, the couple had a son who was given the name of Constantine. Then Constantius, already one of the most notable generals of the empire, received the sudden and perhaps unexpected order of Diocletian. With it there came the bitter hour for Helena's departure, leaving her place to an unknown princess whom the political plans of Diocletian had destined for Constantius.

Thus the former *stabularia* returned again to the shadows. Her son, Constantine, who was then about twenty years old, was far away. Born the son of a brilliant officer, and growing up in that rugged province of Illyria which for a half-century had furnished the best troops of the empire, Helena's son could not be anything but a soldier, and in fact he enrolled in Diocletian's army and fought during those years under the command of his emperor in Egypt.

Constantius Chlorus followed his own destiny. He married Theodora, he fought valiantly in Gaul and in Britain, and had many legitimate children by his princely wife. Far away and forgotten, Helena, his mistress of other times, led her obscure life. Constantine, attaining manhood, fought in Asia and Africa, thousands of miles away from the provinces governed by his father. For the illegitimate son of Chlorus and his mother, history seemed to have nothing extraordinary in store.

6. Step-daughter of the Augustus Maximian.

7. She was probably born about A.D. 248 or 249. The date of Helena's birth, however, like the dates of her death and of the birth of her son, is extremely controversial.

8. Today Niš, in Yugoslavia.

9. It is to be hoped that it was not for this reason that her celebrated son promulgated the law *Cod. Theodos.* 9.7.1 in A.D. 326 which, more for contempt than compassion, exempted the tavern-girls and their slaves from the law De Adulteriis.

But in less than fourteen months every reasonable expectation was overturned by three unexpected events.

The first of these was the double abdication of Diocletian and Maximian. On the same day and at the same hour in their seats of Nicomedia and Milan, the two Augusti who for twenty years had governed the empire in harmony removed the purple before their massed troops. This was May 1, A.D. 305. In east and west, the mechanism of the succession operated simultaneously. The two Caesars, Galerius and Constantius Chlorus, became Augusti.

The second event which occurred unexpectedly to change the destiny of Helena's son was the invitation which Constantine received to join the father who seemed to have forgotten him and whom he had not seen for twelve years. With reluctance, and in that climate of suspicion which preceded the collapse of the Diocletianic system and the spread of civil war, Galerius, at whose court Constantine was stationed, had to permit his young officer to depart. At night, and before the appointed hour, Constantine fled from the perfidious palace of Nicomedia and after a long and fantastic ride across Asia Minor and Europe joined his father at Gessoriacum[10] on the Atlantic coast, at the very moment that the latter was embarking for Britain. Thus, after thirteen years of separation, Constantius Chlorus embraced his lost son, and in so doing stirred up memories of his youth, while Constantine, his cold-blooded ambition sharpened by long years of exile, saw for the first time on the shoulders of his failing and tired father the reflection of the shadow of supreme power. His wait was not to be long. On July 25, A.D. 306, on his return from a brief campaign against the barbarians of Scotland, the emperor of the west closed his eyes in the imperial palace of York. And this was the third event of that extraordinary year.

10. Today Boulogne-sur-Mer in France.

The legitimate issue of Constantius and Theodora were still children, and Constantine was present in the camp at York. He must have been, at thirty-three, a fine figure of a man and a decisively able officer. Moreover, from the first moment of his arrival at the west, Chlorus had kept him always at his side, almost as if he wished tacitly to recommend this long-neglected son to his soldiers. The acclamation of Constantine as Imperator Augustus was thus the last fatal link in this exceptional chain of events. Hardly fourteen months had passed since the abdication of Diocletian. Far away, at Spalato, in the quiet of his magnificent palace by the sea, the old emperor saw the beginning of the collapse of that delicate system of succession which was to have prevented the empire's falling into the recurrent tragedy of civil war.

Our purpose here is not to narrate the bloody intricacies of alliances, wars and betrayals which during a period of eighteen years brought Constantine from the palace of York to absolute dominion over the entire Roman world. But it is interesting to note how the shadow of his mother Helena appears behind the shoulders of this cruel and intelligent emperor from the beginning of his great adventure. The care, one might dare to say tenderness, with which a pitiless and calculating prince like Constantine covered his mother with honors illuminates an unexpectedly human side of the son of Constantius Chlorus. Certainly in Constantine's soul the same psychological mechanism was at work that over two centuries before had set off the pathological affection of Caligula for all the members of his unfortunate family. The long years in obscurity, frustrations and sense of injustice had joined the mother and son indissolubly. From her exalted, honored and venerated station, Helena was to exercise as time passed an increasingly great influence over her son. Behind the triumph of Christianity one sees the shadow of this powerful woman who was the first openly Christian Augusta, and in the dark tragedy which in a few years was to rock the family of Constantine we may divine the unsettling presence of the former *stabularia* of Niš.

The first coin portraits of this perplexing woman appear on folles[11] coined possibly between A.D. 315 and 323. These were years in which Constantine, having solidified his domination over the west, prepared for the decisive encounter with Licinius, the last of his rivals. The face of Helena, who at this time must have been about seventy years old, appears on the small bronze coin illustrated in Plate LXI with fair characterization of her features despite the stylistic tendencies of the period. There is no trace of the massive geometric quality of the coin portrait of the tetrarchy. The hardened and decayed profile is that of a woman who, if not seventy, is certainly advanced in years. In the prominent and slightly aquiline nose, the hard and straight mouth, and the almost vertical line of the forehead we recognize, in an aged state, the profile of Helena in her beautiful marble portrait in the Capitoline Museum in Rome. But above all we find in the expression of the mother certain unmistakable traits of Constantine's. To recognize these it is enough to consider the magnificent portrait of the emperor on the solidus [12] of Plate LXI.

The hairdressing is of the very simplest; it almost seems negligent. The hair, divided by a part in the center of the head, falls in two soft masses to the nape of the neck where it is gathered in a small knot. About this portrait, so little courtly and yet so effective, there is a similarly simple legend: HELENA N F[13]. Nobilissima femina: this was the honorific title given by Constantine to his mother on his accession to the throne. Later, in 324, when Constantine was sole master of the immense empire after the defeat of Licinius, the title of Augusta was conferred on Helena, and from that moment on her head appeared on coins wearing the imperial diadem.

It is in the years between A.D. 324 and 329[14] that the aged Augusta exercised her greatest influence on her imperial son and dominated the imperial scene. At that advanced age, when in the sunset of life men withdraw into themselves in search of a tranquillity which is the almost certain omen of death, Helena lived the greatest moment of her earthly existence. It was a grandeur, note well, that was iron-willed, pitiless determination, never a reverberation of others' glory but a simple reflection of the power of Constantine. But this was also a grandeur made dark and muddy through an obscure tragedy which the reticence and self-serving silence of the Christian hagiographers succeed in veiling, though not in hiding completely.

The theatre of the drama was the court of Constantine. The protagonists are the emperor himself, his son Crispus, his young stepmother Fausta and the aged Helena.

In 326 Crispus, the twenty-six-year-old son Constantine had fathered on a concubine in his youth, was accused by Fausta, the young wife of the emperor,

11. See note 4 of this chapter.

12. Between A.D. 310 and 312, in the western provinces under his control, and in 324 over the whole empire, Constantine had the weight of the gold coin (aureus) diminished by one-fifth, reducing it to 1/72 of a pound, that is, 4.54 gm. The new coin, issued in great quantity, was accepted immediately because of the purity of the metal and accuracy of its weight. It was called the solidus, and was subsequently the fundamental coin of the Byzantine empire during the entire high middle ages.

13. Helena Nobilissima Femina (Helena, noblest of women).

14. The probable date of her death.

of an attempt on her virtue. Outraged at the presumed treachery of his son, Constantine ordered the execution of the traitor when the court was in Rome for the twentieth anniversary of his reign. But Crispus, who had fought bravely with his father in the recent civil wars, was too popular. To execute him in Rome would be imprudent. And so privately and without publicity the prisoner was taken to Istria, and there the terrible sentence was furtively executed.

But the aged Helena, who had not been able to avert this terrible bloodshed, discovered, little by little, the truth. It was Fausta that, like some new Phaedra, her advances refused by Crispus, had desired to avenge herself by slandering him. The duel between the two women was brief and ruthless. Under the powerful pressure of maternal influence, Constantine began to feel that he had committed a terrible error. It was in this climate, already poisoned by suspicion, that the discovery of an affair, actual or invented, between Fausta and a slave gave Helena the opportunity for the revenge she had so long desired. A few months after the assassination of Crispus Fausta, the last daughter of the great Maximian, was strangled in her bath by imperial order.

This is the version of the facts which, amid a thousand reticences, contradictions and intentional ambiguities is furnished by the ancient authors employed to portray the protector of the Church as a severe but just monarch and his mother as a saint, vindictive perhaps but always illuminated by the message of Christianity.

Too many centuries have passed since this obscure drama. We do not know, and probably shall never know, if the ancient tragedy of Hippolytus and Phaedra repeated itself in the palace of Constantine. It may be that Crispus, handsome, young, and bold and, what counted more, popular among the troops, had conspired against his father. And it is probable that Fausta, whether she were or were not the primary cause of the ruin of her stepson, would have looked with pleasure on the death of a man older than her own sons who blocked their future possession of the empire. But, whatever the facts, the gratitude and praise that for two thousand years has been lavished on the first protector of the Christian church cannot obliterate the bare atrocity of the facts. Crispus did not stand alone before the executioner. Together with him there was brought to "justice" the son of Constantine's sister [15], Licinianus, a boy hardly fifteen years old, whose only crime was to have had Licinius, Constantine's former rival, for a father [16]. With the fall of Crispus, the three sons of Fausta enjoyed the role of hereditary prince which had belonged to their brilliant illegitimate brother. Three youthful Caesars [17] now were approaching the throne of Constantine, the father who had killed their mother, their grandfather [18], their uncle [19], and their half-brother.

No posthumous exaltation can remove the stains of this horrendous sequence of crimes. No license of sanctity can absolve the former tavern-girl of Niš from the responsibility of having been the influential counsellor of such a son.

We can see the features of Fausta, the perplexing and mysterious witness of so many horrors and perhaps the sinister protagonist of the drama of Crispus, on a coin illustrated in Plate LXII, a very rare solidus struck, with all probability,

15. Constantia, daughter of Constantius Chlorus and Theodora, was, to put the case exactly, the half-sister of the emperor.

16. Licinius surrendered to Constantine in A.D. 324, after the battle of Chrysopolis. Constantine pretended to pardon him but after a few months had him assassinated at Salonika where Licinius was being detained.

17. The three sons of Fausta and Constantine were born in A.D. 316, 317 and 323.

18. Maximian, father of Fausta, was assassinated by Constantine in 310 after having been taken prisoner.

19. Maxentius, son of Maximian and brother of Fausta, died in 312 during the battle against Constantine at the Milvian Bridge near Rome.

between A.D. 324 and 325. Her father, Maximian, the man who had divided the empire with Diocletian for twenty years, could not adapt himself to the retirement which had been forced upon him by his colleague in the east. He had therefore left his beautiful villa in Lucania and plunged into the civil wars which followed the fatal announcement of A.D. 305. In A.D. 307, Maximian had married Fausta, his youngest daughter, to the thirty-four-year-old Constantine. That unconscious living pledge of alliance was then nine years old.

At the time when the coin we are examining was struck, Fausta was at most twenty-seven years old and her earthly existence was coming rapidly to its tragic conclusion. If we are to believe the historians, there was already burning in her soul the flame which shortly would bring down Crispus and herself. But the face of the young Augusta appears totally expressionless. In the plump and immobile features of the wife of Constantine we search in vain for a trace of the passion which stirred her or for a sign of the terrible experiences through which she lived. In this lifeless face the round and open eye betrays, beneath the tired figurative shell of the image, the eruption of new tendencies now turning towards depersonalization of portraits and towards the abstract stylization of the human face. Only the hair is still alive. In the soft, undulating mass of the hair and in the tight knot behind the nape of the neck from which a few rebel locks protrude, we recognize once again the care, rather I would say the inspiration, with which the engravers of Roman dies always described the hairstyles of the Augustae. However, the type which appears on the reverse of this coin (Plate LXIII) is certainly more interesting than the anonymous face of Fausta. In a representation in which the still-classical composition is in strange contrast to the medieval flavor of anatomical deformation, the empress appears in a standing pose, holding two of her three sons in her arms[20]. Around the symbolic type the legend SALUS REI PUBLICAE (Salvation of the Republic) echoes motives of dynastic propaganda which we have already encountered on other imperial coins. Our thoughts run to the childish faces of Geta and Caracalla which regard each other on the coin of Plate XXXIX. Hopes and human ambitions were destined to break up against a reality often crueler than any that can be imagined. One of the two children in Fausta's arms was to fall by his brother's hand, the other was to have a long but inglorious reign. And the woman who carries them was to die by assassination a few years or perhaps a few months after the issue of this coin.

20. Constantine II and Constantius II, proclaimed Caesars in 317 and 323 respectively. The youngest son of Fausta, Constans, is not shown on the coin because at the time at which it was struck he had not yet been proclaimed Caesar as had his brothers.

With the death of Fausta, no barrier stood between the spirit of the terrible old woman and that of Constantine. Revered, feared, and surrounded by a halo of almost mystical respect, Helena, the incomparable stage manager of her own life, wished that its last act would be worthy of her dizzying rise. New Rome, the fine city which, as if by magic, was rising on the banks of the Bosphorus, planned and conceived by Constantine as an eternal sign of his power, was already full of her statues. In her honor Drepanum, a city of Bithynia, had changed its name to Helenopolis. But all this was not enough. If the pagan empresses had been divinized *post-mortem,* the first Christian Augusta would have her apotheosis while alive.

Helena was already eighty when the magnificent cortege that was to escort her to Jerusalem set out from Constantinople. In the twilight of her life the empress was crowning her adventurous career on earth with the pilgrimage to holy places of the new faith.

The long voyage which should have been inspired by Christian simplicity was transformed step by step into an apotheosis of the pilgrim. Wherever she passed prisoners were pardoned, the poor were aided and exiles recalled. New churches marked the route of her passage. But the old lioness had not lost her claws. These were the years of the furious struggle between the Arians and the Orthodox, and Helena was surely not a woman to limit her activity to pious works and sacred ritual. A fanatic Arian, she deposed, as she passed Antioch, Eustatius, the bishop of that city, who was guilty of being aligned on the other side of the argument. Then finally, after a long voyage, the regal cortege reached Jerusalem.

The story of the discovery of the cross is too well-known to recount here[21]. It is certain that the episode was not the first example of that flourishing industry in relics which in the space of a few centuries was to fill the world with tons of fragments of the true cross and hundreds of nails of the crucifixion as well as dozens of portraits of the Madonna painted by St. Luke or by the angels in person. And nevertheless we should recognize that at this moment Bishop Macarius showed a far from common commercial instinct. Agreeing with the eternal principle that for an exceptional client one should reserve exceptional treatment, the enterprising prelate saw to it that from the bowels of Calvary and before the eyes of the octogenarian empress there was exhumed a relic of the most regal quality: the true cross on which Jesus was crucified, intact, naturally, complete with nails and with a label explicity and legibly bearing the inscription INRI (the initials of *Iesus Nazarenus Rex Judaeorum,* Jesus of Nazareth, King of the Jews).

21. Out of respect for truth it may be useful to recall that the story of the discovery of the true cross by St. Helena may be a legend which sprang up at the end of the fourth century. It does seem strange that the leading panegyrist of Constantine, Eusebius of Caesarea, and other Christian chroniclers of the time make no mention of it. Extensive accounts are given, however, by St. John Chrysostom in 390 and St. Ambrose in 395, not without contradictory elements.

From his regal client Macarius received all that he planned for. There was money in profusion, magnificent donations, and fully twenty-eight basilicas built in all the holy places of Palestine. But once again it was the former *stabularia* of Niš who derived the greater advantage from this extraordinary operation. What coronation of her long and fortunate life could have been more triumphant than this? With the discovery of the true cross, Helena left the narrow limits of history to enter Christian legend.

The return from the mystic voyage was slow and solemn. The fiber of the old Augusta was still strong, but night was coming on. On a day and in a place that we do not know, Helena closed her eyes forever. She had been cynical, equivocal, and pitiless. But she had protected the Church and had made it powerful. Through her effort the persecuted Christians had become the persecutors. This was no little achievement. For future generations, the mother of Constantine would be St. Helena.

We shall bring this chapter to a close by describing a coin which, if not the last, was certainly one of the last struck in the name and in the honor of Helena. Up to now, we have talked about portraits. But it is not the ravaged face of an old woman that we find on the splendid gold medallion of Plate LX. Her head bound with the imperial diadem, Helena appears transfigured in the image of youthful beauty. It is the very image of regal majesty rather than a portrait which leaps out at us from this coin. The heavy stylization and plebeian taste of the epoch of the tetrarchs have given way to a courtly and aristocratic elegance already explicitly Byzantine. Moreover, in this stupendous image of the young Helena we find the same characteristics and the same undefined fascination of the best coin portraits of her imperial son (Plate LXI below). In both coins the relief of the image has lost its traditional prominence and has become very low. In the general flattening of the features the dramatic light and shade effect so dear to the Roman engravers of an earlier time disappears and the entire representation assumes the tone of an exquisite but slightly cold calligraphic exercise. The engraver, now more graphic artist than sculptor, likes to draw the undulating mass of the hair with minute refinement and takes pleasure in expanding on the oriental richness of the diadem while losing himself in describing the thick folds of the drapery. Within the frame provided by this magnificent work of the engravers, there is nonetheless a structure and expression of the faces which in these two coins reaches the culminating moment of transition between two civilizations and between two artistic and spiritually opposite points of view. The faces of Helena and of Constantine are not yet the anonymous symbols which in a short time become habitual in Byzantine coinage. In them, in a refined and transfigured form though it be, we still recognize the facial traits of two real and living persons. But none-theless in the images of the emperor and his mother we find, above and beyond the physiognomic precision with which the personages are represented, a completely Byzantine and medieval concept of portraiture which aims at representing the idea impersonated by the individual in place of the individual himself. And no one in the world can deny that, not only on their coins but also in their lives, Helena and her son represented two grandiose even if awe-inspiring "images of royalty".

Chapter 9

# THE HOUSE OF THEODOSIUS

## Aelia Flaccilla: the Obscure Wife of Theodosius.

1. May 22, A.D. 337.

2. January 19, A.D. 379.

Between the death of Constantine[1] and the accession to the throne of Theodosius[2] forty-two years intervened. This almost half-century was full of dramatic events, wars, usurpations. Beginning with the bloody family feud among the many heirs of Constantine, this tormented period saw the long and inglorious reign of Constantius II, the brief adventure of Julian the Apostate, and the rise and development of the new Valentinian dynasty. These are the years that mark the final triumph of the Christian revolution, a triumph halted only for an instant by the aristocratic pagan dream of Julian the Apostate.

In the forty years that divide the reigns of the two emperors to whom posterity gave the title "The Great", Roman coins pass down a facial record of the protagonists of history but never those of their wives. There is no female portrait to testify to the existence of the women of Constantius II, Julian, Valentinian, and the other emperors of this period.

We must reach the family of Theodosius to find the last great female figures of the empire. And, once again, there are coins to give us the facial features of the last Augustae of Rome.

3. This was the highest rank in the military hierarchy of the period.

4. Now Edirne, in Turkish Thrace.

The first of these empresses was Flaccilla. The Spaniard Theodosius married her when he was still a minor officer brought up in the hard school of his father, the most prominent general of the entire period. Then one of the many obscure intrigues of the palace so common at this time implicated the old *magister equitum*[3]. After his father's execution, the son was permitted the favor of retiring to the vast estates which his family possessed in Spain. There, between Vallodolid and Segovia, the young ex-officer led the quiet and retiring life of a country gentleman for three years. Then he received the sudden and unexpected call which was to transform his destiny. On August 9, A.D. 378, Valens, the brother to whom Valentinian had entrusted the eastern part of the empire, had attacked a great army of Goths, Huns and Alani, under the walls of Adrianople[4]. In a terrible battle the Roman army was routed. It was a military disaster which could be compared only with the battle of Cannae. The emperor himself fell fighting among his troops. While the barbarians camped beneath the walls of Constantinople the nineteen-year-old Gratian, a nephew of the dead Valens and emperor of the west, finding it impossible to confront the situation alone, in the gravity of the hour called the talented officer that he himself had exiled to far-off Spain to govern the eastern provinces. Through an extraordinary combination of fortunes, the thirty-three-year-old Theodosius received the imperial purple from the hands of a man who only three years before had killed his father.

Thus began the adventure of this great emperor, an adventure which in a little more than a decade was to lead to the domination of the entire empire from the

Pillars of Hercules to the Black Sea. And over this great dominion the Theodosian dynasty was to rule for almost eighty years.

Of Flaccilla, overshadowed by the personality of her great husband, we know almost nothing. And yet she must have had some influence on the emperor if it is true that on the one occasion when Theodosius seems to have accepted an invitation to a debate made by an Arian bishop it was the prayers of his wife which made him cancel the appointment, which could have opened a dangerous crack in his monolithic orthodoxy. And this was not an isolated case. In fact, it is interesting to note how all or almost all of the imperial women in the period of the tetrarchs are shown to be at first fervid supporters, then zealots and often fanatic members of the new religion. It is clear that the suggestion of Christianity exercised a potent influence on feminine irrationality and no historian can ever say with certainty what silent but powerful contribution toward the triumph of the new religion was made in intimate family conversations by women like Prisca, Valeria, Helena, Constantia, Fausta and Flaccilla.

However this may be, the face of the wife of Theodosius appears on a majorina[5] coined between A.D. 383 and 395, the year in which the Augusta died. The first thing which strikes us as we look at this image (Plate LXIV above) is its expression of aristocratic refinement. The precious beaded necklace, the magnificent pendant earrings and the rich and complicated, almost crownlike diadem harmonize perfectly with the proud expression on her face. It is a face more of a *Basilissa* (Greek for queen) than of an Augusta, a far and distant personification of power, radiant with gems and with gold. At the same time, however, it is a face in which we seem to catch a trace still of personal physiognomy in the form of the mouth, the fullness of the cheeks and the expression of the large and slightly protruding eyes. We have the same reaction as in the case of the image of her husband on the solidus of Plate LXIV where we may believe we recognize the facial traits of the great Theodosius, even though reflected in the exaggerating mirror of the stylistic taste of the period which preferred elongated faces and despite the strong tendency towards abstraction in the elegantly refined, almost Byzantine court style.

5. A bronze coin introduced by Constantius II and by Constans about 346 in place of the follis which had already been reduced to a small bronze coin of very little value.

Aelia Flaccilla was not the only wife of Theodosius, and Arcadius and Honorius, two sons who divided the empire at his death, were not his only heirs. After the death of Flaccilla, the emperor married Galla, a young daughter of Valentinian, and by her he had a daughter, Galla Placidia, who was to become wife and mother of emperors. In the following paragraphs we shall recount the adventurous life of this woman and the no less incredible adventures of her daughter, Honoria, and of her daughter-in-law, Eudoxia II.

## Visigoths, Huns and Vandals: the Sad Fate of the Last Augustae of the West.

If a writer of fiction were to inquire which of the great personages of Roman history would be most readily adapted to the colorful genre of an adventure story, he would not hesitate to choose the queen whose remains perhaps rest

6. It is not at all certain that the so-called Mausoleum of Galla Placidia at Ravenna ever contained the mortal remains of the Roman empress. In conscious contrast to the severe simplicity of the exterior, the vault, the lunettes of the lower arch and the dome of this interesting tomb are covered with mosaics with a copper blue background, flaming with green and gold like the starry heavens.

under the star-studded vault of the beautiful mausoleum at Ravenna [6]. But if a writer of a more intimate turn should ask us the name of the imperial princess who more than any other had played out the eighteenth-century myth of the romantic heroine in the events of her life, we could point out none other than Honoria, the unfortunate daughter of the great Galla Placidia.

The story of these two women took place in that part of the empire which may be defined quite properly as the empire of the west. Mighty centrifugal forces of a crisis that had lasted for centuries in the immense Roman state had done their work for over a century to split apart the empire in which every cohesive force seemed to be dissolving into nothing.

Diocletian was the first to understand that if the state were to survive it was necessary to divide the west from the east, at least in fact if not officially. After him, the changing turns of history had brought the empire to unification more than once under the guidance of great men. But Constantine, Julian and Theodosius had been able to halt the inexorable flow of history only for an instant. Renewed at various times by the sons of Constantine and by Valerian, the division of the empire had always respected the Diocletianic arrangement of a hierarchy of two Augusti which preserved, formally at least, the conception of a united empire. But when Theodosius died on January 19, A. D. 395, without leaving precise orders in his will, even this last tenuous formal barrier fell. The empire was for the first time officially divided between Arcadius and Honorius. The West and the East separated their destinies forever.

On that winter day the west set out on a new path, one that was never again to meet that of the Mediterranean Orient. And thus there came to an end a long era of human history.

Settled in the melancholy city on the marshes to which fear and ineptitude had driven him, Honorius passively lived out the slow death of the realm that chance had given him. Waves of Vandals, Suevi, Burgundians, Alani and Goths brushed by Ravenna which remained secure among the marsh canals, a fit capital for a decomposing state. Barbarian guards, Alani and Goths, defended the emperor in his impregnable stronghold.

It was in 408 that the Goths, commanded by the legendary leader Alaric, laid siege to Rome for the first time. The year following, with the punctuality of a periodic calamity, Gothic hordes appeared again before the ancient, terrorized capital. Finally, on August 24, A.D. 410, Rome was assaulted and stormed. "Eleven hundred and sixty-three years after the foundation of Rome, the Imperial City, which had subdued and civilized so considerable a part of mankind, was delivered to the licentious fury of the tribes of Germany and Scythia" [7].

7. Edward Gibbon, *History of the Decline and Fall of the Roman Empire,* London 1813, Vol 5, Chapter 31, page 311.

The adventures of Galla Placidia begin at this moment. Educated at the court of Constantinople, the daughter of Theodosius and Galla had followed her half-brother west but not to his secluded city fortress on the Adriatic. Remaining at Rome, the twenty-year-old sister of the emperor was taken prisoner together with thousands of other unfortunates during the terrible sack of the city.

Galla Placidia was then in the flower of her youth. Most ancient authors, with the sole exception of the Goth Jordanes, say that she was not particularly beautiful. But for the barbarians into whose hands she had fallen, the fascination of the imperial prisoner was something more than that of physical beauty. She was the daughter of a great emperor, and they had taken her, together with that mythical capital of the world on which the Germans had looked for centuries as an unobtainable prey. Galla Placidia was a symbol of the weak and decadent world that they could devastate and destroy but the immense superiority of whose civilization they also vaguely felt.

Alaric, the king who had conquered Rome, knew how to defend himself from this fascination for that small span of life that remained to him. After six days of sack, he left the city behind him and, wreaking devastation in his path, marched south through Campania and Calabria to the Straits of Messina. Beyond this small arm of the sea there lay the last untouched goal, Sicily. But, overcome by a sudden illness, Alaric was never to reach Sicily. Jordanes, in *De Rebus Geticis*, tells of the funeral of the hero of his people, how as in a Nibelungen saga a throng of prisoners deviated the Busentus[8] from its course. A tomb was dug in the bed of the river to receive Alaric and his trophies. Then the waters of the river were brought back to their natural bed. All the prisoners who had executed this work were killed so that the site of the sepulchre would remain forever unknown. Finally, the Goths broke camp and slowly took their way back across a devastated Italy. Far from his nomadic people, far from the din of battle, Alaric now lay in his inaccessible tomb at the bottom of the river.

8. A small river that flowed beneath the walls of Cosenza.

We cannot say if what we have narrated is true history or only a legend born in the night around the campfire. But readers who perhaps still remember the verses of Platen and of Carducci[9] will pardon our having told it.

9. The tomb in the Busentus inspired more than one artist. A. von Platen wrote a ballad on the subject which Carducci translated in *Rime Nuove.*

Galla Placidia, who as a prisoner had followed the Gothic army to Calabria, felt at that moment, perhaps for the first time in her life, the fascination of that youthful people. How different were these warrior-kings from her unwarlike brother! No one would ever have dug Honorius's tomb beneath the swift waters of a river. The emperor of the west had already buried himself alive amid the swamps of Ravenna.

For his part, Athaulf, the young king who succeeded Alaric in ruling the Goths, could not free himself from the fascination of the royal daughter of Theodosius. During the slow retreat along the flaming peninsula, Athaulf married Placidia. A hundred trays full of gold and gems captured in Italy were the splendid wedding present of the new queen of the Goths.

From that moment on, Galla Placidia exercised an ascendancy over her husband which was to determine every one of his military actions. Through the charm of a woman, the dying empire of the west was to find its most powerful ally and the fresh military energies of Athaulf's people were to be ever more frequently employed in the defense of the throne of the vacillating Honorius. In 414, Athaulf led his restless people to conquer Spain which had been in a state of confusion for years due to the invasion of the Alans and the Vandals. With him were Galla Placidia and Theodosius, their small son. The death of this child seems to have foreshadowed the tragic end of his father. In Barcelona, the same city where the little son of the Gothic king and the Roman princess was buried in a silver casket, Athaulf fell before the assassin Singericus.

This was a private vendetta and the usurper held the throne for only a week, but for Placidia they were seven terrible days. The daughter of the great Theodosius was menaced and brutally maltreated by the once-again hostile hordes. In the meantime, in far-off Constantinople, the death of her husband was celebrated with games and displays of lights.

With the death of the usurper and the proclamation of a new king, Galla Placidia once more had respect and security, if nothing else. But the enchantment that had bound her to that proud people was broken forever. For Galla Placidia, the Goths returned to being a savage horde, hostile to the name of Rome. And for Wallia, the new king of the Goths, the sister of Honorius again became a precious hostage from the imperial court. In the meantime, the weak forces of the western empire had found in the Roman Constantius one of those brilliant captains whom exhausted nations sometimes can bring forth in an extreme crisis. The troops of Constantius quickly blocked the passes of the Pyrenees. Reduced to hunger, Wallia and his people, having devastated the land of Spain [10], could neither return to the north nor properly face the Vandals who still held a great part of the Iberian peninsula. In these circumstances there was no choice but to accept the conditions of the Roman general: 600,000 measures of grain immediately, and the promise of regular shipments of grain in the future, in exchange for Galla Placidia and the assistance of the Goths in Spain under the sovereignty of Honorius.

10. The Vandals of Spain made fun of the Goths by calling them "Truli" because in their desperate situation they were ready to trade a gold coin for a *trula,* that is to say for approximately a half pound of flour.

The pact was signed. After five years of adventures among the barbarians, Galla Placidia returned to her own people. Constantius, her unloved liberator, asked her hand in marriage and obtained this prize for his victories from Honorius a short time later, on January 1, A.D. 417.

By means of this marriage, which Placidia accepted without enthusiasm, the fortunate general placed a mortgage on the throne of the west and soon the birth of a child, Honoria, and then in 419 a son, the future Valentinian III, further reinforced Constantius's position.

Finally, in 421, Honorius, who was childless, decided to take the man who had served him so well in war as a colleague. Galla Placidia had the title of Augusta and the small Valentinian that of Nobilissimus, which practically designated him as successor to the throne.

It seemed now that after so many vicissitudes Placidia might expect some peace and tranquillity, but this was not to be. Without warning, Constantius died after a brief illness. Only seven months had elapsed since Honorius accepted him as an equal on the throne. And once again Placidia had to live the bitter and difficult life of a widowed queen. Surely in those days the phantoms of the terrible week in Barcelona returned to the mind of the daughter of Theodosius. But Ravenna was not the Gothic camp of Athaulf, nor was the kind of menace that could come from a man like Honorius clear and brutal like that of Singericus. At first, however, nothing seemed to upset the relations of brother and sister. Then, if we can believe the historians of the period, Honorius's affection for this sister who had been lost and found again transformed itself, little by little, into an ambivalent passion.

Placidia then retired with her two children to Rome. Visiting the great city in decadence certainly disturbed her, and the traces of the Gothic sack were still visible everywhere. Enclosed in the useless circuit of the Aurelian walls, the city had a spectral air. Some of the great monuments of the past had fallen. Gardens and other cultivated plots spread inside the walls where formerly there had been populous quarters. Wind-carried seeds covered walls and reliefs with grass and wild flowers.

Placidia certainly revisited the palace from which she had been dragged by main force so many years before. In that petrified city where the sky, the trees, the walls brought forward memories of impotence and fright, the sister of Honorius felt herself caught in a trap. In secret and at night, taking her children with her, she left Rome and embarked on the first ship leaving for Constantinople. Fleeing her own memories perhaps more than the hypothetical designs of her brother, she thus reached the great city spread out on the banks of the Bosphorus.

She was received by two other notable women of whom we shall have more to say, Pulcheria, the austere sister of Theodosius II, and Eudocia (Athenais), his young and beautiful wife. And when, after a few months, Honorius died unexpectedly and the throne fell into the hands of a usurper, the armies of the east in two years of warfare reconquered the western empire for Placidia and her small son [11].

11. August 27, A.D. 423.

Before Constantius's widow embarked again for Ravenna, the three women who ruled the fate of the empire decided to sanction their alliance through an engagement. The small Licinia Eudoxia, the daughter born to Eudocia only three years before, became the promised bride of Galla Placidia's son, who was barely seven years of age. Twelve years later, the promise would be faithfully kept [12].

12. Licinia Eudoxia was born in A.D. 422, Valentinian in A.D. 419.

Thus, at thirty-five years of age, the widow of Athaulf and of Constantius came to govern the confused empire of the west in the name of a child. Fifteen years of adventures had not broken the exceptional fibre of the last daughter of Theodosius. Rather, the misfortunes and dangers of a life spent in the tents of nomads and in the court of Ravenna had always proven the character of this woman to be stronger than that of the men who possessed her body. From the moment of their marriage to the hour of his death, Athaulf had fought practically in the service of the emperor who had never dared to meet him in open battle. And if this fact were not sufficient in itself, it suffices to read the account of the wedding feast described by Olympiodorus at which the king of the Goths appeared in Roman dress seated on a modest chair while Placidia is described as seated on a magnificent throne and resplendent in all the robes of a Roman empress. Such an account makes one understand how the ferocious victor was conquered by his royal prisoner.

After Athaulf, Constantius was also dominated by the personality of the young woman who had been ransomed for 600,000 measures of grain and whom Honorius had given him as a reward for his political and military successes. Once again, in fact, Placidia had known how to rebel against that recurrent vile destiny which made her a mere victor's prize and to raise herself to be the architect of her own fortune as well as that of her husband and her sons.

Certainly, in Honorius's decision to accept Constantius with him on the throne we recognize the final act of the wise maneuvers of the daughter of Theodosius.

After her elevation to the throne, Galla Placidia governed the west for twenty-five years[13]. The power which twice she had attained and twice lost never again deserted her, not even when the weak and corrupt Valentinian III reached his majority.

13. From A.D. 425 to November 27, A.D. 450, the date of her death.

These are the years of her rare coin portraits. The face of the daughter of Theodosius that appears on the few coins where the features have not been abstracted into anonymous idealization is that of a mature woman, with strongly marked features, a full throat and a hard mouth (Plate LXV). From on high a heavenly hand reaches out to crown the head of the empress of the west, an image typically Byzantine in feeling and conception[14]. The hairstyle is still that of Flaccilla, but is even more abundantly adorned with precious stones and pearls. The long and heavy braid that rises like a helmet-crest from the nape of the neck to the forehead disappears almost completely under a heavy, formal diadem. Everywhere — in the hair, on the neck, on her robe — there is a rain of precious stones. Viewing the barbaric splendor of the hairdressing and robes of the last Roman Augustae, Placidia, her daughter Honoria, and her daughter-in-law Licinia Eudoxia, one's thoughts turn to the unadorned simplicity of the hairstyles of Livia and Antonia. One cannot help but think what power was hidden behind their simplicity, and how much incurable weakness was masked behind the splendor of these others.

14. The head of the empress crowned by the hand of God appears for the first time about A.D. 400 on solidi struck in the name of Aelia Eudoxia, wife of the eastern emperor Arcadius. The same allegorical type appears thereafter on solidi struck in the name of Eudocia, Pulcheria, Galla Placidia and Honoria (see Plates LXIX, LXV and LXVI).

Galla Placidia died at sixty in the city of Rome where, fifty years before, she had begun her adventures. The date was November 27, A.D. 450. She left her thirty-one-year-old son, a stupid degenerate finally at liberty to ruin himself completely, and a daughter of thirty-three years of age, Honoria, whom her mother had sent to a convent at Rome or Ravenna.

This daughter, as we have seen, was the first child of Constantius and Placidia[15]. Raised at the court of Ravenna, the granddaughter of Theodosius had been honored with the title of Augusta at an early age, and in all probability was encouraged to make her vow of perpetual virginity while still extremely young.

15. She was born in A.D. 417.

It was probably for this last reason that serious and irreparable scandal occurred when the sixteen-year-old became pregnant. The father, who belonged to the retinue of the imperial family, was immediately killed. It is not difficult to imagine that the girl rebelled with all the energy of her youth against the violence done to her affections and the object of her love.

But Galla Placidia was not a woman of half measures. To squelch the scandal it was necessary to send her daughter away from court forever. So Honoria was put on board ship and sent in exile to Constantinople, with instructions to her eastern relatives to keep her constantly under close surveillance.

The personages who received her were those least willing to heal the wounds of a young, disturbed girl. Theodosius II, the emperor, was a bigot who spent his nights in copying over and over, one does not know whether for pleasure or penitence, the New Testament in tiny characters of gold, the text on every page written in the form of a cross. He excelled in this strange exercise, so much so that he was called "The Calligrapher". His sister Pulcheria, seven years older than he, was the true mistress of the empire. Born thirty-five years earlier in Constantinople, she too, like the rebel who was now entrusted to her care, had made a solemn vow of virginity, and the words of her oath were still written in gold and precious stones on the great altar table that she had dedicated to God in the cathedral of Hagia Sophia.

Delivered into the iron grasp of this woman of inflexible devotion, Honoria began her long period of expiation. For twelve, perhaps for fourteen years, the daughter of Galla Placidia lived in a semi-prison permeated by rigid and intransigent piety. Still, the years went by. In A.D. 437 her brother came to Constantinople to claim the wife that had been promised him when he was a child. Valentinian III was then eighteen years old, Licinia Eudoxia, his bride, was a beautiful adolescent of fourteen or fifteen years of age. From her gloomy prison the twenty-year-old Honoria saw the city filled with illumination and festivities in honor of the couple, and perhaps harbored in her heart the illusion of returning to Ravenna in the suite of her more fortunate brother. But when this hope, too, was deluded, Honoria understood that for her there would never be pardon, and that the cloistered life against which she rebelled with her whole spirit would not end before she died. Perhaps it was in this moment that the daughter of Placidia began her desperate search for a means, any means, of escape. And with the passage of time this longing for liberty and perhaps also for revenge became an obsession which would lead Honoria to take the most desperate of decisions.

The name of Attila was famous and feared in Constantinople. Frequent embassies maintained contact between the encampment of the savage king of the Huns and the imperial palace. It was through one of these that Honoria succeeded in sending her ring to the barbarian chieftain with the request that he ask her hand in marriage and, if her relatives refused, that he come and claim her and with her that part of the kingdom which was hers by right. From his wooden city on the Danube, Attila replied demanding of Theodosius II the hand of Honoria and her inheritance[16].

The demand left the court at Constantinople astonished. Then the reaction of Theodosius II and Pulcheria took form in the only action possible. Placidia's daughter was immediately put on board ship and sent back to Ravenna, and with her Attila's dangerous matrimonial request was sent to Valentinian III.

It was only through the intercession of Placidia that Honoria, though guilty of having brought the attention of an enemy such as this on the empire, escaped death. But before hiding her forever in a prison or a convent, Valentinian had her quickly married to an obscure nominal husband in order to provide a pretext for his refusal of Attila's request.

But the train of events that Honoria's desperation had set in motion could not be halted so easily. The king of the Huns requested her hand twice, and twice, upon its refusal, invaded and devastated the western empire. In A.D. 451 it was Gaul's turn and the destruction was terrible. Defeated at Châlons, the leader of the Huns retired, but a year later invaded the empire again, and on this occasion systematically destroyed the cities of northern Italy. Valentinian III, fleeing from Ravenna to Rome, capitulated quickly. Pope Leo was sent to

16. The adventures of Honoria are recounted in a confused version in the *De Rebus Geticis* of Jordanes and in the *Chronicles* of Prosperus and Marcellinus. According to some modern historians (Stein, for example, in his *Histoire du bas Empire*), Placidia's daughter suffered her disgrace when she was already thirty-two years old. The appeal to Attila would thus have been launched immediately after the death of her mother. In this treatment of the story, however, we remain faithful to the version of the facts given, among others, by Gibbon and Gregorovius.

meet the Scourge of God and the Roman embassy which accompanied the bishop of Rome bought the safety of the capital from Attila with the promise of finally handing over to him Honoria and an immense dowry.

In her prison, the unfortunate daughter of Placidia saw within her grasp at last that liberty which she had sought and dreamed of with such tenacity for twenty years. But fate still held in store for her the most tragic of her disappointments. A few months before the day appointed for her departure, Attila suddenly died of a haemorrhage. Every one of Honoria's hopes collapsed. No one would mention her again, even to record her death.

Time has not preserved for us any other portrait of the unfortunate daughter of Galla Placidia save that minted on a few gold coins issued in her name before disgrace overtook her. We would expect, therefore, the portrait of a young girl, hardly more than an adolescent, but the stylistic tendencies of the period, united with the limited ability of the engraver, disappoint any hope of knowing the true features of the unfortunate princess. Perhaps none of the portraits of the Augustae we have described up to now is as general and anonymous as that illustrated in Plate LXVI. Under the rich hairdressing typical of the imperial ladies of this period there appears a totally impersonal face, so stylized that it is difficult to determine the age of the subject. The large, protruding eyes, the large, straight nose, the generalized set of the mouth and of the cheek show the progress of stylistic tendencies which find their fulfillment in the perfect geometric schematization of certain faces of the high Byzantine era. But, while other coin portraits of this period show the abandonment of Roman realism as a means to the transfiguration of the face in a symbolic ideal of royalty, the depersonalization of the face of Honoria is merely a sign of the incapacity of the artist.

Just as inept stylistically but far more interesting as a document of a delicate moment of transition between two civilizations is the reverse of this coin (Plate LXVII). It bears a winged Victory, one of the most common artistic subjects of pagan Rome, but on the solidus of Ravenna the Victory of the Caesars carries the cross of Christ. And in the mingling of the symbols of the ancient religion and the new faith, we find an unintended allegory: the massive adoption of pagan anthropomorphism by the Christian religion which, perpetuated through the centuries, was to constitute the most evident external difference between the religion of Christ and its original Judaic mold.

Galla Placidia was dead, Honoria had been buried in a dungeon, but in the imperial palace of Ravenna there still lived a woman of the family of Theodosius, Licinia Eudoxia. Licinia Eudoxia was the eldest daughter of the western emperor Theodosius II and the fascinating Eudocia. She was the pretty girl who, in far-off days of the years before, had appeared to the unhappy Honoria almost as a symbol of that felicity which she had been denied forever. Since that long-past day on which the eighteen-year-old emperor of the east had come to Constantinople for her, many years had passed and many illusions had gone. Valentinian III had shown himself a nonentity. For thirteen years, the new empress had been forced to submit to the authority of her mother-in-law, who was determined to leave to her lazy and vice-ridden son nothing but formal power. Then, after the death of Galla Placidia, Valentinian III, now deprived of that tie and also of that substantial support represented by his mother, had sunk more and more into corrupt inertia.

But Eudoxia had never given up loving the husband whom reasons of state had destined for her when she was still a child. Fundamentally, her life had proved as much determinated as Placidia's or Honoria's, but while the strong personality of her mother-in-law had been able to bend every chance and every circumstance to her favor, and while desperation had led her sister-in-law to dare everything, Eudoxia was not able to detach herself emotionally from a husband who was so unworthy of her. This was not foolishness, as we shall see, but one of those mysterious psychological mechanisms that so often indissolubly bind worthy individuals to the unworthy.

The assassination of Aetius, the courageous general who had defeated Attila at Châlons, was the first of a series of useless and despicable acts which in a short time transformed universal disapproval of Valentinian III into bitter hatred. The last of these acts was the rape by the thirty-six-year-old emperor of the wife of Maximus, a senator belonging to one of the most powerful Roman families. On March 16, A.D. 455, while he was attending military maneuvers in the Campus Martius, the last emperor of the family of Theodosius fell under the daggers of those whom he had offended and injured. Maximus himself, the organizer of the plot, was immediately invested by the senate and the troops with the imperial purple. Perhaps out of a spirit of revenge, perhaps to consolidate his position, Maximus committed an error from which his own sad personal experience, if nothing else, should have deterred him. He forced the widow of Valentinian to marry him. It was, therefore, the same hateful abuse that ruined his predecessor which destroyed him after hardly three months' reign.

For Licinia Eudoxia, in that moment, there was only one ambition: to avenge the death of Valentinian and free herself from a man who repelled her. No help could reach her from Constantinople, her fatherland. Her father, Theodosius II, and her aunt, the great Pulcheria, were dead. Her mother, now retired from political life, had lived for years in exile in Jerusalem and on the throne of the east there was now seated a man she did not know. But before Eudoxia's eyes there was a recent and terrible example, Honoria. Attila was dead, but another barbarian no less famous than he had established himself with all his people on the shores of Africa. This was Genseric.

To believe ancient sources, it was to him that Eudoxia turned in secret to ask aid. The coup which had failed Honoria by a breath succeeded for Eudoxia. But the facts show that this apprentice sorceress had evoked fearful and uncontrollable forces. The Vandal fleet, leaving Carthage on June 12, A.D. 455, anchored at the mouth of the Tiber. In the city, amid a turmoil of fear, in the profound calm of the three days that preceded the assault of the Vandals and the desert tribes accompanying them, Eudoxia must have tasted the honey of that private vendetta for which she had loosed forces so ruinous for her own country. Maximus, seized by a terrified mob and betrayed by his own mercenaries while attempting flight, was butchered and thrown into the Tiber. But Genseric had not come to give justice to an injured woman, nor to vindicate an emperor whom in fact he had never known. His aim was only a gigantic raid and he acted for this purpose. For two weeks, from June 15 to June 29, A.D. 455, Rome was given over to sack and devastation. Eudoxia, solely responsible for the disaster, was captured with her two young daughters while she was making her way to her liberator. Robbed of her jewels, she was treated like any other prisoner, embarked and carried with so many hundred other guiltless unfortunates to Africa.

The expiation suffered by the widow of Valentinian was long and painful. She remained for seven years in the hands of the Vandals. Only in A.D. 462, following a peace treaty between the eastern emperor Leo and Genseric, were Eudoxia and her younger daughter Placidia given back to the civilized world. But the other daughter, Eudocia, was forced to marry Hunneric, the eldest son of the Vandal king, and to remain at Carthage. It was only in A.D. 471, after sixteen long years as a prisoner, that she succeeded in fleeing to Constantinople.

Of Eudoxia, the last feminine protagonist of the dramatic history of the western empire, there exists a single fascinating coin portrait struck in gold on rare solidi coined in her honor in Rome and at Ravenna [17]. For the first time in the coin iconography of the Roman Augustae the face and bust are shown in frontal view, following a tendency which was destined to become dominant in the Byzantine period (Plate LXX). But already in this exceptional representation there is nothing, absolutely nothing, of concrete Roman realism. The hieratically fixed expression of the face, crowned with a cascade of gems, the barbaric sumptuousness of the diadem set with rays and surmounted by a cross, the fluid outline of the shoulders under the criss-crossed folds of her mantle reflect a civilization in which the values of transcendental Christianity have a preponderant weight and are reflected in an artistic style as far as possible removed from the world of common appearance.

A hundred years later, in the same city, another artist of genius was to portray in the brilliant colors of a celebrated mosaic another *Basilissa* whose life was full of adventures, Theodora [18]. In the pallid face of the wife of Justinian weighted down by a heavy diadem of pearls we recognize the strange transfiguration of human corporeality into a symbol of hieratic majesty which characterizes the less well-known but no less fascinating coin portrait of Licinia Eudoxia. The same rigid frontal pose given by the unknown artist to the face of the wife of Valentinian III also characterizes the reverse type of this fascinating coin (Plate LXXI). It is again the Augusta who appears here in full frontal pose, seated on a throne. It is a figure of abstract royalty which holds in her right hand a cross-topped orb and in her left hand a long sceptre. Disposed around the figure, the legend SALUS REI PUBLICAE rings in our ears with a macabre irony. No one could have thought that one day the submissive spouse of Valentinian would sacrifice to a private vendetta the state of which she should have been the bulwark of salvation.

With the career of Licinia Eudoxia and her emblematic portrait a long period in the story of the west comes to an end. Five hundred years after its beginning, the Roman empire was dissolving forever under the powerful attack of new people without history. The intertwining of the destiny of the last three Augustae of the west with that of the three barbarian kings most

17. These solidi were struck during the reign of Valentinian III.

18. The famous mosaic showing Theodora and her court is at Ravenna on the wall of the apse of the Basilica of San Vitale. A masterpiece of Byzantine mosaic art, it was executed in A.D. 547 together with the panel which decorates the other sidewall of this apse and which shows her husband, Justinian, surrounded by ministers, ecclesiastics, and soldiers. The fascinating portrait of Theodora calls to mind the older portrait of Eudoxia not only because of the conscious idealization present in both these images but also because of the striking and almost identically sumptuous hairstyles of the two Augustae.

feared and abhorred by the Romans seems, to the historian, like a symptom of the extreme decay of the entire world. But in the dramatic adventures of Placidia and Athaulf, of Honoria and Attila, and Eudoxia and Genseric, we may also recognize the seed which after a long winter of devastation and barbarism would generate a new people and a new civilization. Ties between the last Roman empresses and the chiefs of the Goths, the Huns and the Vandals reveal that slow and grandiose process of assimilation which was already at work among the anonymous masses of the humble people of whom history never speaks. By this ethnic fusion between victors and vanquished, one day, a new and different western civilization would be reborn.

## In the East: Aelia Eudoxia and her Enemy.

If Galla Placidia, Honoria and Licinia Eudoxia marked the last agonizing throes of the western empire with their personality and their fatal decisions, three other exceptional women characterized the contemporary history of the empire of the east.

Today, Aelia Eudoxia, Pulcheria and Athenais are forgotten names, unknown even to the majority of educated persons. The story of the women who bore these names, like that of Placidia, Honoria and Licinia Eudoxia, is lost among the colorless pages of arid Byzantine epitomes. But during their lives it was they and not the weak menfolk who bore the imperial title who dominated, for good or for evil, the stage of the Roman world.

Let us leave forever, therefore, Rome and Ravenna and, going back some years in time, betake ourselves to the magnificent city on the Bosphorus, capital of the eastern empire, which, born on January 19, A.D. 395, was to outlive the western empire by a millennium.

Arcadius, the elder brother of Honorius, was eighteen when he mounted the throne of Constantinople in A.D. 395 and was only thirty-one when he died on May 1, A.D. 408. His brief and insignificant life was dominated in turn by an intriguing eunuch and a beautiful and unscrupulous wife, Aelia Eudoxia [19].

The elder son of Theodosius had married her on the 27th of April, A.D. 395, only three months after the death of his father. As often happens in royal families, the marriage between the young and weak emperor and the pretty orphan daughter of Bauto [20] was, at the beginning, a mere episode in the internal battles of the courtiers of the imperial house. The choice of this bride pressed upon the young emperor by his counsellors was meant to topple a very important but hated minister who hoped to marry his own daughter to Arcadius.

The hidden objective of the marriage was realized. Rufinus, the minister, who had clouded the last years of the reign of Theodosius with his abuses and whom the lazy Arcadius had accepted as part of his paternal inheritance, fell and in his place there appeared the equally unworthy courtier who had plotted his misfortune, the eunuch Eutropius.

19. Not to be confused with Licinia Eudoxia, about whom we have spoken in discussing the events of the western empire and who was Aelia Eudoxia's niece.

20. Bauto was a brave Frankish general who had fought in the service of Rome. After his death, his daughter, Aelia Eudoxia, was brought up in the home of another famous general named Promotus.

What no one foresaw, however, was that the young bride would not be content with the role of a mere presence beside her colorless husband. Absolute mistress of her husband's spirit, Aelia Eudoxia has been described by ancient writers as a resolute, unprejudiced, ravishingly beautiful woman. And the coins with her name that still have a trace of the ancient sensitivity of the Roman portraitist seem to confirm all the subtle charm of the first-ranking Augusta of the east (Plate LXVIII). Under the sophisticated hairdressing which clearly recalls that of her mother-in-law Flaccilla[21], there appear the young features of Eudoxia, a fine but not thin face posed on a long neck *à la Boldini,* a straight forehead, small nose, a small mouth, slightly creased in a smile *da Gioconda* which varies between the enigmatic and the ironic. Hers is an aristocratic expression, and at the same time one of zest and spirit which instantly recalls to mind the portrait of the young bride of Marcus Aurelius that we illustrate in Plate XXX.

21. See Plate LXIV above.

A woman of this sort could certainly not be content to be the docile companion of an insignificant man like Arcadius. Nonetheless, the action of Aelia Eudoxia would have been no different than that of so many other intriguing and faithless women whom we have encountered in these pages if fate and the spirit of the times had not matched her as enemy against the most celebrated, perhaps, of the patriarchs of Constantinople, John, called Chrysostom[22] because of his sweeping eloquence.

22. "Golden Mouth."

Born at Antioch, a seething religious center, John Chrysostom belonged to that class of the faithful whose primary virtue was an iron will tovards themselves and others. From its beginning his life had been that of a pure though violent champion of the faith. Educated by his rich and noble family at the school of the sophist Libanius, one of the most famous pagan orators of the time[23], John, like so many young men of his day, had felt the new and irresistible fascination of the religion of Christ. He then gave up everything and retired to the Syrian desert. In the solitude of that lunar landscape, among privations which are impossible for us to conceive, the brilliant lawyer of Antioch sought God for six long years. Sickness forced him to return to his city, but the experience of the desert had marked him forever. Returned to the world of the living, John Chrysostom dedicated the eloquence whose arts he had learned in the pagan schools to the service of his burning faith. And it was the magical powers of his voice that brought him to the episcopal chair of Constantinople in A.D. 398.

23. Libanius had been the teacher of the emperor Julian the Apostate. His influence on the rhetoric of John Chrysostom was enormous.

In that grand and restless city the violent intransigence of the former hermit opened bloody wounds and fired secret hatred. The magical voice that enchanted the crowd each Sunday from the pulpit of Hagia Sophia fell like a sword on the peak of two pyramids of power. His pastoral visit to the provinces of Asia sowed resentment and fear. From city to city the archbishop passed like an avenging angel. On his return one could count thirteen bishops of Lydia and Phrygia deposed for simony or improper life. And those remaining trembled in the knowledge that Chrysostom had publicly declared that the number of bishops who could be saved was far smaller than those who would be damned[24].

24. *Homilies,* 3.

If John had shown himself without pity to unworthy religious, in the life of the court the implacable archbishop found material all too easy for his burning sermons and his harsh warnings. The entire world of elegant frivolous women who moved about the beautiful empress was exposed without pity to public reproof. Then, through transparent metaphors, the inquisitorial fury of the saint was turned against the highest and most dangerous objective, Aelia Eudoxia.

The duel between the archbishop and the empress was brief and dramatic. Around Eudoxia, whom Chrysostom called Jezebel in his sermons, there collected all of those forces whose safety depended on the ruin of John Chrysostom. In A.D. 403, in a synod held in the neighbourhood of the capital itself[25], forty-five bishops signed the condemnation of the proud patriarch who had refused to attend. Theophilus, the archbishop of Alexandria, had been the soul of the conspiracy, but behind him there was visible the shadow of the wife of Arcadius.

25. At Chalcedon, on the Asiatic shore of the Bosphorus.

Neither Theophilus nor Eudoxia had appraised properly the scope of the passions excited by the stormy oratory of the former hermit. After a brief moment of amazement, John's arrest sparked bloody riots in the capital. The people dimly understood that by silencing Chrysostom privilege was again using force to silence truth. And the rebellion of the common people showed the court for the first time the danger of his immense popularity.

The flight of Theophilus and the capitulation of Arcadius marked a brief triumph for John Chrysostom. The ship carrying him into exile was recalled when it had barely entered the Black Sea, and the archbishop was brought back to his cathedral through an exultant and festally-illuminated city amid the acclamation of the people. In this triumph no one, not even John Chrysostom, thought of annulling the sentence of the synod.

Experience, minimal good sense and the fact that his sentence had not been revoked should have suggested a certain caution to John Chrysostom. But prudence and tolerance were two words unknown to the archbishop. "Herodias is angry again; Herodias is dancing again and calls once more for the head of John." With these now-famous words Chrysostom began the sermon that was to destroy him. On the eve of Easter in A.D. 404, in a city now massively guarded by troops, the enemy of Eudoxia was deposed for the second time. John saw Hagia Sophia for the last time from a ship carrying him to exile. Above the church there rose the dense columns of smoke from the fires set by his desperate followers.

For Chrysostom there was neither return nor pardon. Though confined by Eudoxia's wishes to Cucusus, a remote city among the mountains of Taurus, the indomitable man of God still knew how to direct his followers from afar. Little by little distance and persecution invested that voice with an almost supernatural holiness. In A.D. 404 Eudoxia, his enemy at Constantinople, died while still young. But other and more subtle persecutors remained to carry on the work of Herodias' daughter. The bishops who had so hated and feared him understood that the myth of John was being fed by his distant exile. It was necessary to still once and forever the influence of that voice. Thus, in September A.D. 407, John set out under guard to be transferred to a destination which was oblivion. Across the mountains of eastern Anatolia, in the suffocating heat of late summer, the sixty-year-old bishop was dragged towards the more remote areas of the Black Sea. The instructions of his guards were clear and were zealously observed. On September 14 death freed John at Comana Pontica, a small city some days' journey from the Black Sea.

26. January 23, A.D. 438.

Thirty years later[26], at the end of a long triumphal journey, the body of the archbishop of Constantinople was to return to his city. Awaiting him in the very suburb of Chalcedon that had seen the synod condemn John there stood in penitential dress Theodosius II, the son of Arcadius and Aelia Eudoxia his implacable persecutor.

## At the Court of Theodosius II: Pulcheria and Athenais.

The beautiful and voluptuous wife of Arcadius had left, on her death, four daughters and a son.

27. The first-born daughter of Arcadius and Aelia Eudoxia was actually Flaccilla, but she died before her father, so that it was Pulcheria and not Flaccilla who was considered the elder daughter of Theodosius.

When Arcadius died in A.D. 408, only thirty-one years old, Theodosius II was no more than seven years of age and Pulcheria, the eldest of his sisters[27], was only two years older than he. Logically, it should have been Honorius, his uncle, who governed the empire in the name of the minor son of Arcadius. But the weakness of the emperor of the west and the desperate condition of his own realm rendered the most logical solution impossible.

In those delicate years of transition, only the ability and fidelity of a minister saved the eastern branch of the Theodosian dynasty. From A.D. 408 to A.D. 415 the praetorian prefect, Anthemius, held the regency in the name of the young emperor with ability and good sense. But in spite of his providential presence, these were years of cold isolation for the orphans of Eudoxia. In the great palace which had become suddenly too empty and too silent a clique of priests taught Pulcheria, Theodosius, Arcadia and Marina the rigid duties of their rank and the fears of an oppressive and ferocious religion. News of the world reached that cold palace attenuated and in fragments. An army of the Huns, conquered by Roman arms, had abandoned Thrace. A new city wall rose like a crown around Constantinople. The construction of warships that were to guard the Danube was undertaken. One day at the end of the summer a piece of news more important than the others seemed brusquely to interrupt the even passage of time. Rome, the ancient, far-off capital, had been stormed by the Goths. And in the immense human and material booty Alaric had carried away a young aunt whom these children had never known, Galla Placidia. It was the end of August, 410. Pulcheria was eleven years old, Theodosius nine.

The rigid and austere education and lack of affection, the lack of a proper childhood, all left their mark on the four children. It made of the boy, weak and uncertain like all the male descendants of Theodosius, a bigoted slave of the church. It made an instransigent and fanatic saint of the intelligent and strong Pulcheria. It made of the two younger daughters two creatures quaking before the Lord and destined to be propelled by the overwhelming example of their elder sister into a life of monastic chastity, fasting and prayer.

28. The sister of Theodosius was, in fact, canonized. Today the Catholic Church holds her feast on the 10th of September.

29. The Nestorians, who hated Pulcheria for her inexorable opposition to their heresies, accused her of being the mistress of a fascinating *magister officiorum,* Paulinus, and of having had an incestuous affair with her brother. It is impossible for us to know whether such accusations are well-founded or are the slander of fanatic enemies. The latter and more serious of these accusations seems to us difficult to believe, however, especially considering the nature, character and life of Theodosius. Since it comes from the same source, the accusation concerning her supposed relation with Paulinus is also probably slanderous.

But Pulcheria was not only a saint[28] dedicated to meditation and good works. As often happens to a family of children who have lost their parents, the older sister became in some way the mother of the future emperor and of her younger sisters. Rapidly maturing by force of tragedy, it was she who, when still a girl, taught Theodosius how to bear himself, speak and receive in public. And the boy, overwhelmed by the clear intelligence and strong personality of his sister, surrendered himself to that sweet tutelage for his entire life.

On July 4, A.D. 414, the boy emperor conferred the title of Augusta on the fifteen-year-old Pulcheria. It was the first recognition of a power already all-too-clearly manifest but which, despite some periods of eclipse, was to last forty years, to the death of Theodosius and beyond. Driven by a mystic fervor that astonishes anyone who remembers the very different propensities of her mother, while still young Pulcheria made a solemn vow of perpetual virginity. And, since her two younger sisters did the same, we can imagine that it was the strong character of Pulcheria and the magical power emanating from her which drove Arcadia and Marina as children to imitate her example. In the presence of the clergy and the people, the three daughters of Aelia Eudoxia consecrated their virginity to God in the same church under whose arches there had echoed a few years before the destructive words of St. John Chrysostom.

Their palace, in which one day the unfortunate Honoria was to be imprisoned, became a convent from which Pulcheria governed in the name of her brother or opposed with varying fortunes the powerful eunuchs of the court. When Theodosius II died without heirs in A.D. 450, it was still she in her old age who courageously took the reins of power in her hands. And knowing full well the intrigues that would inevitably surround a woman alone on the throne, Pulcheria did not hesitate to choose, in the person of an aged senator Marcianus, a husband who would respect her vow and would at the same time be capable of sharing with her the responsibilities and the duties of supreme power.

Coins show us the face of this woman whose clear intelligence could combine the difficult art of governing with a burning spiritual flame[29]. With her rather prominent nose and small, insignificant chin, Pulcheria, at least as far as one can see on the solidus illustrated in Plate LXIX above, did not have the spirited beauty of her mother or the subtle fascination of the other woman who marked the epoch of Theodosius with her romantic story: Athenais. The portrait of this princess, born a pagan in Athens and to die a Christian in Jerusalem, will be the last of the portraits of the Augustae which we shall examine in this book. With her, the last empress to have been born and brought up in the ancient faith of the gods, the history of the classical world comes definitively to an end and there begins the long era of medieval Byzantium. In her fortunes, contained in the brief space of the years of one human life, there seems to be a synthesis emblematic of all that long evolution of the spirit which led the Graeco-Roman world from the concrete rationality of paganism to the ecstatic mysteries and bitter theological discords of early Christianity.

Athenais, the daughter of the sophist Leontius, was born at Athens, probably about A.D. 400. The old capital of classical culture was by this time reduced to a small provincial city. "Cunctos populos in tali volumus religione versari, quam divum Petrum Apostolum tradidisse Religio usque ad nunc ab ipso insinuata declarat."[30] The words of the first edict by which Theodosius the Great ordered that all the people of the empire profess the religion of Peter made certain a decay already in motion for some time. Other decrees followed. The surviving pagans were forbidden to sacrifice to their gods. Every word and every line hid some incitement to violence against the last followers of the ancient faith. Then, in A.D. 395, the Gothic invasion of Alaric, coming with the fury of a cataclysm, caused chaos from one end to the other of Greece, and though Athens, by paying ransom, had been able to escape the horrors of a sack, around her all Attica, from Cape Sounion to Megara, was devastated by the barbarian hordes. The splendid paintings of Polygnotus which had ornamented the Stoa for centuries disappeared, stolen by one of the numerous rapacious proconsuls sent out by Constantinople. Finally, on June 9, A.D. 408, the emperors Arcadius and Honorius promulgated by a severe edict orders that the statues of the gods should be removed from those temples that had not yet been destroyed, that the pagan altars should be overturned, and that the sacred buildings which had escaped the fury of the Christians should be given over to secular use.

30. *Codex Theodosianus,* 16, 1-2. (We wish all peoples to be gathered in that faith which declares its establishment and continuation by Peter, prince of the Apostles).

It was in this atmosphere of slow decay that little Athenais grew up. And though the imperial edicts were in part circumvented in the ancient stronghold of paganism[31], the feeling of belonging to a condemned minority with no escape penetrated profoundly in the sensitive soul of the child. In that somnolent city of the provinces, moreover, every day news of the rest of the world was brought by ships coming from the populous centers of Africa and Asia, Alexandria, Antioch and Constantinople. There was news of temples destroyed, odious discrimination, and Christian violence. On the Acropolis and the Parthenon the great chryselephantine statue of Athena looked over her city still. But for how long?

31. Not only in Athens, but in all Greece, ancient beliefs survived tenaciously. Proof is given by the fact that from the fourth century on the term "Hellene" became synonymous with "pagan" in common parlance.

Leontius imperturbably carried out the education of his daughter according to the customs of those last exponents of pagan Greek culture. In the small world of Athens, among so many memories of the past, Athenais, who had become a beautiful girl, studied grammar, rhetoric, mathematics, music and poetry. She read the ancient texts of great Greek culture: Homer, Aeschylus, Thucydides. She learned, like all the noble ladies of her day, to weave gold and purple garments.

The years passed quickly. At Constantinople Pulcheria was reigning in the name of her brother Theodosius II. When Leontius, in an unknown year, died, that comfortable provincial life came to an abrupt end for Athenais. In his will the old philosopher left all his modest estate to his two sons, and for his daughter only a sentence: "I wish that my dear daughter Athenais be given one hundred gold pieces because she has in herself already sufficient felicity to outstrip that of any lady."[32]

32. Malalas, 14.353. The same in the *Paschal Chronicle* and in later Byzantine historians.

Athenais was plunged unexpectedly into poverty. After a dispute with her brothers, the young woman left her paternal home and went to live with a maternal aunt. For a number of months, perhaps for some years, she remained in Athens seeking to promote her hopeless case. Then with her aunt she went to Constantinople to a Christian sister of Leontius. It was A.D. 420. In the hope of finally obtaining justice, Athenais, on the advice of her paternal aunt, who perhaps had been introduced at court, asked an audience of the young Augusta, and that encounter changed her life.

Theodosius II was already a young man of nineteen years of age, and Pulcheria in her farsighted wisdom understood that the time had come for her bigoted and inexperienced brother to marry and perpetuate the dynasty. In the young Athenian girl of his own age far more than in the girls of that lugubrious court Pulcheria recognized the beautiful, cultivated, intelligent woman worthy through and through of becoming the wife of an emperor. Even Paulinus, the handsome youth who was the close friend and counselor of Theodosius, found the "Achaean" fascinating and urged a union.

The ancient world did not have the social prejudices of our day. The middle-class background of Athenais was no problem, just as Arcadius had found no problem in the barbarian origins of his wife Aelia Eudoxia. Pulcheria's description of the girl, moreover, immediately inflamed the heart of Theodosius. And, as in a fable, the provincial girl who had come to the capital seeking justice was introduced into that sumptuous court, presented to ministers and to that melancholy young man who had never seen her before. Theodosius II was overcome by the beauty and culture of the Athenian girl, and perhaps Athenais felt a sad fascination for that young man with his blond hair and his large dark eyes. In A.D. 421 the wedding was solemnly celebrated before the court and the clergy of Constantinople. A short time before, the daughter of Leontius had abjured the faith of her forebears. Atticus, the archbishop of the capital, had baptized her with the name Eudocia, and according to Greek custom Pulcheria, the architect of her fortune, had adopted the new follower of the one true God [33].

The years in Athens were now far away, almost unreal. The old gods appeared useless statues of stone. Athenais had overcome the barrier which separated the survivors of a defeated and persecuted religion from the multitude of followers of the Church triumphant. Never did she look back. Not even in A.D. 423, when a new imperial edict condemned to death all the pagans guilty of sacrificing to the gods. Not in A.D. 426, when another edict ordered the destruction of the temples or their transformation into Christian churches. In the palace on the Bosphorus the girl of Athens was dead. In her stead Eudocia composed a history of Christ and his miracles in Homeric verse.

In 422 the beautiful wife of Theodosius II gave birth to a daughter who was given the name of her paternal grandmother, a name which seemed to hold and synthesize in its meaning all of the hopes of the young couple, Eudoxia [34]. Theodosius then gave his wife the title Augusta. The star of the new empress shone beside that of Pulcheria, but it was always the latter who silently kept true power.

The summer of 423 was marked by the arrival of an illustrious exile. Fleeing from Rome, Galla Placidia, the last adventurous daughter of the great Theodosius, aroused the curiosity of a court which with the arrival of Eudocia had found once again the lustre and brilliance of other times. While the war which was to bring Placidia to the throne of the west was being meditated, the two Augustae of the east had the opportunity of meeting that extraordinary

33. In Greek the word "eudokia" means "benevolence" or "favorableness".

34. The word "eudoxia" means "glory" in Greek.

woman who lived through the tragic hours of the sack of Rome and had shown that she knew how to live in the tents of the barbarians just as much as in the imperial palace of Ravenna. The feeling between these three exceptional women must have been spontaneous and sincere, because before leaving they promised to unite in marriage one day the children that constituted the hope of the two empires, Valentinian III and the young Licinia Eudoxia.

These are the years in which we find the first coin portraits of Eudocia (Plate LXIX below). Their generic images are impersonalized like so many other coin portraits of the period. We shall look in vain under the hairdressing, heavy as a helmet, for something more than an anonymously attractive face. The Roman coins that so often have handed down unforgettable portraits of insignificant or unknown women have nothing to offer of the fascinating Athenais except this stereotyped image, a fresh and youthful expression, a straight nose, and a pretty mouth. This is all. The face of Athenais, in its true image, we do not and perhaps never shall know.

Meanwhile, the years were passing. About A.D. 434 another exile from the west disembarked on the marble pier of the royal port. Honoria, at seventeen, began her long expiation, cherishing rancor and vain hopes. Three years later there came from Ravenna the eighteen-year-old Valentinian III to claim the bride who had been promised him as a child. For days the city went wild with lights, festivities and music. Then Licinia Eudoxia, the one daughter of Athenais, set out to her new capital. She was only fourteen years old.

Eudocia's star reached its high point in those years. In a time of burning religiosity, the power of the new faith had overcome the soul of the former pagan like magic. The empress was then thirty-eight years old, an age that represents in the life of every woman a delicate moment of transition between youth and maturity. In her life, as in a fable, everything had been won. Now, as if in a pause for reflection, the Christian convert felt the deep desire to know those places where that God whom she had misunderstood and denied for so many years had become flesh for the salvation of mankind.

On January 23, A.D. 438, on one of those chilly winter days when the wind from the steppes blows through the straits and sweeps the streets of Constantinople, the ashes of St. John Chrysostom returned from exile to the city that had denied and banished him. At Chalcedon, on the Asiatic shore, the emperor, prostrate before the casket, implored pardon for his guilty parents. Then, across the white-capped waters of the Bosphorus, the body of John Chrysostom was slowly carried to the church of the Apostles. Silent crowds followed the ship on both banks while all the church bells of Constantinople sounded together. In the face of this apotheosis, Eudocia's desires were transformed to decision and became a vow.

In the spring of the same year, with an immense suite, the Augusta set out for Jerusalem. Never since St. Helena had a Roman empress undertaken a pilgrimage to the Holy Land. The long voyage was slow and festive. At Antioch the pilgrim paused. Before the senate of the city, seated on a throne of gold set with gems, Eudocia made a speech of classical elegance which ended with a verse from Homer: "This my glory, to be one of your race and your blood." [35]

35. This detail is recounted by Evagrius (1, ch. 20).

Not all of the world repudiated twenty years before had been forgotten. And then, finally, she reached the Holy Land.

Jerusalem, which Helena had visited a hundred years before, had remained in essence a small, dusty provincial city full of memories of the old empress who, before dying, had wished to see with her own eyes the land of Jesus. The former devotee of Athena remained there no less than a year, lodged, probably, in a monastery. She saw the holy places of her new faith, Nazareth, Bethlehem, Cana, Tiberias, and was profoundly touched. Around her Palestine broke into a new flower of new churches, chapels and monasteries. Even the relic industry found in her burning enthusiasm an undiscerning and generous client. The right arm of St. Stephen, an authentic portrait of the Madonna painted by St. Luke, and the two chains with which Herod had bound Peter recompensed the ardent faith of the convert for her long voyage, her rich alms and generous foundations[36].

36. After her return to Constantinople, Eudocia gave one of these two chains to the Church of the Apostles, the shrine where the bones of St. John Chrysostom reposed. She sent the other as a gift to her daughter, Licinia Eudoxia, who built a basilica in Rome to house it, San Pietro in Vincoli.

But the months were quickly passing and it was necessary to return. Leaving Jerusalem, the wife of Theodosius certainly had no suspicion that she would be returning to this city that had bewitched her in a few years as an exile. In the year A.D. 439 Eudocia was once again with her husband in Constantinople.

The pilgrimage to the Holy Land marks perhaps the highest point in the parabola of the life of the empress, but also it is the beginning of her misfortune. The Augusta found the conditions at court almost unchanged. Pulcheria ruled as ever, a watchful and omnipresent shade behind the children of the emperor. Theodosius passed his nights in study and in illuminating the Gospels by the light of a lamp of his own invention which refilled itself automatically with oil. By day, the hunt, his one masculine interest, absorbed his attention completely. Paulinus, his old schoolmate, the brilliant and fascinating man whom Theodosius had always regarded with an admiration typical of the unbalanced towards a friend who did everything with ease, continued to be the influential *magister officiorum*[37].

37. That is, minister of the imperial household.

Everything was as before. But something had changed in the soul of Eudocia. For the first time, separated from the affectionate but iron surveillance of Pulcheria, the wife of Theodosius had tasted, at each stage of her long trip, the intoxicating sensation of absolute power. Though she was the wife of the eastern emperor, mother of the queen in the west, Eudocia accepted again, though with reluctance, the perennial state of subordination which previously she had submissively accepted as a debt of gratitude towards her sister-in-law.

Moreover, a new and unsettling figure moved in the circles of the court. He was the eunuch Chrysaphius, called "Tajuma", who was acquiring an ever-greater hold on the soul of Theodosius. He was one of those sordid individuals who seem to characterize with their intrigues the history of the court of Constantinople, not only in the Byzantine era but also in the centuries of the Ottoman empire. It is therefore possible that a latent rivalry between the two Augustae was purposely exasperated by someone who, like Chrysaphius, had every interest in dividing the spirits of the persons nearest Theodosius. According to rather late sources, Paulinus became the object of an increasing rivalry between the two women. Pulcheria, after a sordid struggle, ceded her

38. Zonaras 3.123, Theophanes 1.151, Nikephorus 14.47.

lover to her more fascinating rival, leaving the imperial palace and retiring to private life in Ebdomon [38].

All these reports, confused, obscure and often contradictory, make it impossible to understand clearly and delineate the true motives for the fall of Eudocia. We know for a fact that there were differences between the two sisters-in-law, and perhaps a sordid struggle. Certainly the former brilliant schoolmate of the emperor played an important role in the fall of Eudocia, probably in her affections and also as a political figure.

39. Two rather important sources for the knowledge of events of this period.

A strange and romantic story in the *Paschal Chronicle* and John Malalas [39] narrates the fall of Eudocia. On the day of the Epiphany in A.D. 440 or A.D. 441, Theodosius went to mass. With him was neither his wife, who had stayed at home, nor his *magister officiorum,* who was kept in bed by an attack of the gout. At the steps of the church a poor man came forward. In his hand he held a magnificent Phrygian apple which he offered to the emperor. Theodosius and his courtiers admired the magnificent fruit, and then the emperor smiled. An order was given and the mendicant received a hundred and fifty gold pieces for the apple which was sent to the palace as a gift for Eudocia. The empress received the fruit and, knowing that Paulinus was sick, sent it to him as a gift. The minister, not knowing from where the fruit originated, thought of arousing the curiosity of the emperor and sent it to him immediately. The circle had closed. Theodosius called Eudocia and asked her what she had done with the magnificent apple that he had sent her a few hours earlier, and the empress, in her embarrassment, not knowing what to reply, said she had eaten it. In the soul of Theodosius perplexity now gave way to suspicion, a suspicion that perhaps had already touched him in the past. Once again he asked Eudocia to tell him in conscience the truth, and the empress, feeling herself now lost, swore she had eaten the accursed present.

We can imagine the state of mind of a man like Theodosius II. For that timid introvert it must have been a terrible disillusionment. So all the fidelity of the wife that he had always adored, the faithfulness of that friend whom he had so much admired was an illusion. Everything now was turning against him, but he still had power and Theodosius used it. Paulinus was put to death, and Eudocia begged and obtained permission to retire forever to Jerusalem.

This is the account of the old Byzantine chroniclers. It is all too evident that the Phrygian apple of Eudocia departs from critical history no more and no less than the fruit of Eve in the terrestrial paradise. It could be that the whole episode is a fable, a poetic fantasy, built on an authentic human drama [40]. The story, however, contains nothing that is absolutely impossible, and may have as much truth as the tale of Marie Antoinette's necklace and Cardinal Rohan.

40. A similar episode is narrated in the story of the three apples in *The Thousand and One Nights.*

Eudocia did not leave immediately. It was necessary to avoid scandal as much as possible, and if the exile of the empress and the condemnation of the minister had been simultaneous everyone would have connected these two remarkable facts. There passed several dark months. Then Eudocia set out again on that road which once before, at the height of her fortunes, she had travelled.

From this moment on, news of Eudocia's life is infrequent and fragmentary. We know that her passionate nature and mystical transports of fervor led her to join the Eutychean heresy which, in A.D. 448, was upsetting the eastern church[41], and that even after the Council of Chalcedon had inexorably condemned the monophysite doctrine in A.D. 451, she obstinately kept to her beliefs.

On July 28, A.D. 450, Theodosius died, thrown from his horse during the hunt. Pulcheria was now on the throne. From Constantinople, although she was feeble, she made the conversion of her sister-in-law the last great objective of her declining years. The two ladies exchanged letters. Had personal rivalry ever existed between them, it had been cancelled by the passage of time. The invisible threads of memory bound them together to a departed world which the veil of time made even more sweet. In this renewed contact there was perhaps more initiative and sincerity than the bare reports of the ancient historians would lead one to believe. But Eudocia remained immovably attached to her religious doctrines.

At the wish of Pulcheria, the other members of the family wrote her. Her daughter, far away, her son-in-law, Valentinian, even the two brothers who, thirty-five years before at Athens, had robbed her of her inheritance[42]. From Rome Pope Leo, the man who had halted Attila, added his voice to that of all those who by bending the will of this one woman intended to rob the Eutychean party of its last and most prestigious standard-bearer. But all was in vain.

Pulcheria was not able to reclaim from heresy the soul that so many years before she had taken from the gods of paganism. The "fortress set by God to defend his church", as Leo had called her, died on September 10, A.D. 453, at fifty-four years of age, after having given all her possessions to the poor.

But fate reserved a final blow for Eudocia. On March 16, A.D. 455, Valentinian III fell at Rome, victim of the dagger of conspirators. In far-off Jerusalem Eudocia certainly trembled to think of the destiny of her daughter Licinia Eudoxia, the thirty-two-year-old widow of a despised emperor. Then, in a stupefying succession, news and more frightening news arrived from the west: the forced marriage of her daughter to the assassin of Valentinian, the invasion and sack of Rome by the savage hordes of Genseric, and her daughter, the empress, dragged on board ship and then held among the Vandals in Africa with her young daughters in a band of prisoners, without rights or name.

So Eudocia was in turmoil. And from her misfortune the priests hastened to turn advantage by making it a breach through which to penetrate her consciousness.

The former empress had no more peace. She was told that the collapse of her family, the imprisonment of her daughter and grandchildren among the barbarians, all was the punishment of Heaven for her obstinate opposition to the creed of Chalcedon. They exorted her to placate the Lord by repudiating that heresy that the pope at Rome and the bishops in the east had inexorably condemned. At last, shaken by so many pressures, Eudocia declared to her tormentors that she would place her soul and her doubts in the hands of the most famous man of those who had sought God in the solitude of the desert. Simeon, called Stylites, the most saintly of the hermits of that time, was living far from Jerusalem on a desert mountain in Syria. First a shepherd at Susan[43],

41. Eutyches, archimandrite of Constantinople, and Dioskuros, archbishop of Alexandria, claimed that Christ had only one nature (monophysism), the human component being completely resolved into the divine. Although condemned initially at a synod, the Eutychean theory kept its following thanks to the support of the emperor in the great Council of Ephesus in A.D. 449, in the course of which the bishops who were not monophysites were intimidated and menaced and their leader, Flavianus, the patriarch of Constantinople, was assaulted with such violence that he died three days later. Finally, after the death of Theodosius II, thanks above all to the support of Pulcheria, those who maintained the double nature of Christ prevailed again and the monophysites were condemned and declared heretics at the Council of Chalcedon, the sessions of which were held in October of A.D. 451.

42. In the moment of her triumph Eudocia had pardoned them, raising them to high state positions which they kept even after her fall.

43. In Cilicia.

he had chosen the life of an anchorite in obedience to an innner voice. And after many years' tormented apprenticeship he was successful in winning the palm of a master without rival in the art of asceticism. In his lucid madness, he had removed himself from the lavish homage of penitents by seeking refuge at the top of a high column. There he passed the nights on his knees in prayer, his joined hands extended towards the heavens.

For thirty summers and thirty winters this man of God resisted the sun and the rain on the top of his airy refuge. Crowds of penitents came from as far away as Gaul and Persia to venerate that "burning lamp on a high candelabrum"[44]. Theodosius II had written him years before, imploring his prayers for the divided and injured church.

44. Thus a contemporary, the bishop Theodoretus of Cyrrhus, defined Simeon Stylites.

It was from this man, then, that Eudocia, already conquered by misfortunes, sought a last counsel. Her conversion to the Catholic Church took place in the year A.D. 456, and with her the Eutychean heresy lost its last and most prestigious exponent.

The last years of Eudocia are empty and obscure. Far from the currents of history, isolated from every man of mind or spirit, agonizing over the fortune of her one daughter, she became a woman living past her time. Time had cut every link with her own life. Theodosius, Pulcheria, Valentinian dead; Licinia Eudoxia remained a prisoner of the Vandals.

Cut off, in complete solitude, she immersed herself in works of piety and devotion. The building of ever-new edifices was now her continual preoccupation. She restored the walls of Jerusalem, built cloisters and hospitals for the poor, and raised churches. But even in this she was unfortunate because posterity attributes all these works to the other more illustrious benefactress of the city, St. Helena.

In the twilight years there was reborn in her heart an old vocation, poetry. The language and rhythm of Homer, so dear to her youth, clothed now the beautiful Christian legend of Cyprian and Justina. The circumstances, misfortunes, and sentiment that reigned there were basically the same as she had suffered and experienced. She, the "Achaean" who in Athens had sacrificed to the demons of paganism, now described, through the laborious ascent of the magician Cyprian from the infernal shadows to the light of God, the sacred path of her own soul[45]. Twelve centuries later, Calderon took material from that same legend for his tragedy *El Magico Prodigioso,* without knowing that a Byzantine empress, great of soul, had preceded him in that path.

45. All the poetry of Eudocia has been lost in the course of the centuries. There remains, from the story of Cyprian and Justina, divided according to Phasius in three parts, the first book and a good part of the second.

Athenais, the daughter of the sophist of Athens, Eudocia, the Byzantine empress, died at Jerusalem about A.D. 460. On the point of death, the old Augusta wished once again to affirm by solemn oath her innocence of the tragic end of Paulinus. Her body was buried in the church of Saint Stephen that she herself had had built near Jerusalem. Eleven years later, there came to pray and to die by her deserted tomb a granddaughter who bore the same name. Eudocia, taken at the age of seventeen in the sack of Rome, having fled after sixteen years of prison among the Vandals in Africa, was buried beside the grandmother she had never known.

# BIBLIOGRAPHY

The reader who wishes to pursue a particular interest should look to the *Oxford Classical Dictionary* (2nd ed., 1970) for brief, authoritative articles and useful bibliographies.

SOURCES
In what follows reference will regularly be made to the *Loeb Classical Library* edition of a given author. Where no Loeb edition is available, reference is made to the standard English translation. It should be noted that, in addition to these, the *Penguin Classics* series provides sound translations of the most important classical authors in an inexpensive format which often includes a worthwhile introduction.

## GREEK

PLUTARCH:
*THE LIVES; ed. B. Perrin; Cambridge, Mass., and London 1914-26.*

DIO CASSIUS:
*ROMAN HISTORY; ed. E. Cary; Cambridge, Mass., and London 1914-27.*

THEODOSIUS II:
*CODEX THEODOSIANUS; ed. C. Pharr; Princeton 1952.*

EVAGRIUS SCHOLASTICUS and THEODORETUS OF CYRRHUS:
*A HISTORY OF THE CHURCH; London 1854.*

THEOPHANES:
*CHRONOGRAPHIA; Leipzig-Hildesheim 1883-1963.*

EUSEBIUS OF CAESAREA:
*LIFE OF CONSTANTINE in: E. C. Richardson «Lives of the Nicene and Post-Nicene Fathers»; 1892.*

JOHN MALALAS:
*CHRONICLE OF JOHN MALALAS; ed. M. Spinka and G. Downey; Chicago 1940.*

JORDANES:
*THE GOTHIC HISTORY; ed. Chr. Mierow; Princeton 1915.*

JOHN CHRYSOSTOM:
*COMMENTARY ON ST. JOHN; ed. T. A. Goggin; New York 1957-60; in «The Fathers of the Church», a New Translation series.*

J. P. MIGNE:
*PATROLOGIAE CURSUS COMPLETUS. SERIES GRAECA; Paris 1857-1866 (*JOHN CHRYSOSTOM: *HOMILIES.* JOHN ZONARAS: *HISTORIES.* THEODORETUS OF CYRRHUS: *WORKS. CHRONICON PASCHALE).*

*CORPUS SCRIPTORUM HISTORIAE BYZANTINAE; Bonn 1837 ff (*NIKEPHORUS OF CONSTANTINOPLE: *WORKS.* JOHN MALALAS: *CHRONOGRAPHIA).*

*CORPUS INSCRIPTIONUM GRAECARUM (CIG); Berlin 1825-1877.*

## LATIN

LIVY:
*ed. Foster, Sage, Moore and Schlesinger; Cambridge, Mass., and London 1919-1967.*

SUETONIUS:
*ed. J.C. Rolfe; Cambridge, Mass., and London 1914-1951.*

TACITUS:
*ANNALS; ed. J. C. Moore; Cambridge, Mass., and London 1925-31. HISTORIES; ed. J. Jackson; Cambridge, Mass., and London 1931-37.*

*HISTORIA AUGUSTA; ed. D. Maggie; Cambridge, Mass., and London 1922-32.*

PLINY:
*NATURAL HISTORY; ed. Rackham, Jones and Eichholz; Cambridge, Mass., and London 1942-63.*

OVID:
*ARS AMATORIA; ed. H. H. Mozley; Cambridge, Mass., and London 1939.*

JUVENAL:
*ed. G. C. Ramsay; Cambridge, Mass., and London 1928.*

MARTIAL:
*EPIGRAMS; ed. W. C. A. Ker; Cambridge, Mass., and London 1968.*

*CORPUS INSCRIPTIONUM LATINARUM (CIL); Berlin 1863 ff.*

H. DESSAU:
*INSCRIPTIONES LATINAE SELECTAE (ILS); Berlin 1892-1916.*

## HISTORICAL STUDIES

P. BROWN:
*THE WORLD OF LATE ANTIQUITY; New York 1971.*

J. CARCOPINO:
*DAILY LIFE IN ANCIENT ROME; New Haven 1940.*

L. FRIEDLANDER:
*ROMAN LIFE AND MANNERS UNDER THE EARLY EMPIRE; London 1908-13.*

E. STEIN:
*HISTOIRE DU BAS EMPIRE; Bruges 1959.*

E. GIBBON:
*THE DECLINE AND FALL OF THE ROMAN EMPIRE; London 1813; New York 1932; Chicago 1952.*

R. SYME:
*THE ROMAN REVOLUTION; Oxford 1952.*

R. SEAGER:
*TIBERIUS; London 1972.*

B. H. WARMINGTON:
*NERO: REALITY AND LEGEND; New York and London 1970.*

F. A. GREGOROVIUS:
*THE EMPEROR HADRIAN; London and New York 1898.*

M. GRANT:
*THE TWELVE CAESARS; New York 1975.*

J. BURKHARDT:
*THE AGE OF CONSTANTINE THE GREAT; New York 1949.*

G. FERRERO:
*THE WOMEN OF THE CAESARS; New York and London 1925.*

J. P. V. D. BALSDON:
*ROMAN WOMEN; Oxford 1962.*

J. R. DE SERVIEZ:
*THE ROMAN EMPRESSES; London 1752.*

A. SOLARI, E. PARATORE, A. G. AMATUCCI, A. CALDERINI, S. MAZZARINO :
*DONNE DI ROMA ANTICA, in «Quaderni di Studi Romani»; Rome 1945-46.*

S. E. POMEROY :
*GODDESSES, WHORES, WIVES AND SLAVES ; New York 1975.*

A. WEIGALL :
*THE LIFE AND TIMES OF CLEOPATRA, QUEEN OF EGYPT ; London 1914.*

O. VON WERTHEIMER :
*CLEOPATRA ; London and Philadelphia 1931.*

M. GRANT :
*CLEOPATRA ; New York 1973.*

*CAMBRIDGE MEDIEVAL HISTORY, VOL. IV : THE BYZANTINE EMPIRE ; Cambridge 1966-67.*

F. GREGOROVIUS :
*HISTORY OF THE CITY OF ROME IN THE MIDDLE AGES ; London 1894-1902.*

F. GREGOROVIUS :
*ATHENAIS. GESCHICHTE EINER BYZANTINISCHEN KAISERIN ; Leipzig 1882.*

## NUMISMATICS

J. N. SVORONOS :
ΤΑ ΝΟΜΙΣΜΑΤΑ ΤΟΥ ΚΡΑΤΟΥΣ ΤΩΝ ΠΤΟΛΕΜΑΙΩΝ; *Athens 1904-1908; Vol. I-IV.*

M. VON BAHRFELDT :
*DIE RÖMISCHE GOLDMÜNZENPRÄGUNG WÄHREND DER REPUBLIK UND UNTER AUGUSTUS ; Halle 1923.*

H. A. GRUEBER :
*COINS OF THE ROMAN REPUBLIC IN THE BRITISH MUSEUM ; London 1910.*

E. A. SYDENHAM :
*THE COINAGE OF THE ROMAN REPUBLIC ; London 1952.*

M. H. CRAWFORD :
*ROMAN REPUBLIC COINAGE ; London 1974.*

C. H. V. SUTHERLAND :
*ROMAN COINS ; London 1974.*

H. MATTINGLY :
*ROMAN COINS ; London 1960.*

J. P. C. KENT, B. OVERBECK, A. U. STYLOW, M. HIRMER :
*DIE RÖMISCHE MÜNZE ; Munich 1973.*

B. V. HEAD :
*HISTORIA NUMORUM, II ed.; London 1911.*

H. MATTINGLY, R. A. G. CARSON, and Others :
*COINS OF THE ROMAN EMPIRE IN THE BRITISH MUSEUM (BMC) ; London 1923-67.*

H. MATTINGLY, E. A. SYDENHAM, C. H. V. SUTHERLAND and R. A. G. CARSON :
*THE ROMAN IMPERIAL COINAGE (RIC) ; London 1923 to present.*

H. COHEN :
*DESCRIPTION HISTORIQUE DES MONNAIES FRAPPÉES SOUS L'EMPIRE ROMAIN ; Paris 1880-1892; Vol. I-VIII.*

V. PICOZZI :
*LA MONETAZIONE IMPERIALE ROMANA ; Rome 1966.*

H. SEABY :
*ROMAN SILVER COINS ; London 1952 to present.*

F. GNECCHI :
*I MEDAGLIONI ROMANI ; Milan 1912; Vol. I-III.*

P. L. STRACK :
*UNTERSUCHUNGEN ZUR RÖMISCHEN REICHSPRÄGUNG DES ZWEITES JAHRHUNDERTS ; Stuttgart 1931-37 ; Vol. I-III.*

R. A. G. CARSON, P. V. HILL, J. P. C. KENT :
*LATE ROMAN BRONZE COINAGE ; London 1960.*

J. TOLSTOI :
*MONNAIES BYZANTINES ; St. Petersburg 1912. Vol. I and II.*

J. SABATIER :
*DESCRIPTION GÉNÉRALE DES MONNAIES BYZANTINES ; Paris and London 1862 ; Vol. I and II.*

R. RATTO :
*MONNAIES BYZANTINES ; Auction Lugano 1930.*

F. IMHOOF-BLUMER :
*PORTRÄTKÖPFE AUF RÖMISCHEN MÜNZEN DER REPUBLIK UND DER KAISERZEIT ; Leipzig 1922.*

J. BABELON :
*LE PORTRAIT DANS L'ANTIQUITÉ D'APRÈS LES MONNAIES ; Paris 1942.*

L. BREGLIA :
*L'ARTE ROMANA NELLE MONETE DELL'ETÀ IMPERIALE ; Milan 1968.*

P. FRANKE, M. HIRMER :
*RÖMISCHE KAISERPORTRÄTS IM MÜNZBILD ; Munich 1961.*

A. ALFÖLDI :
*DIE MONARCHISCHE REPRÄSENTATION IM RÖMISCHEN KAISERREICHE ; Darmstadt 1970.*

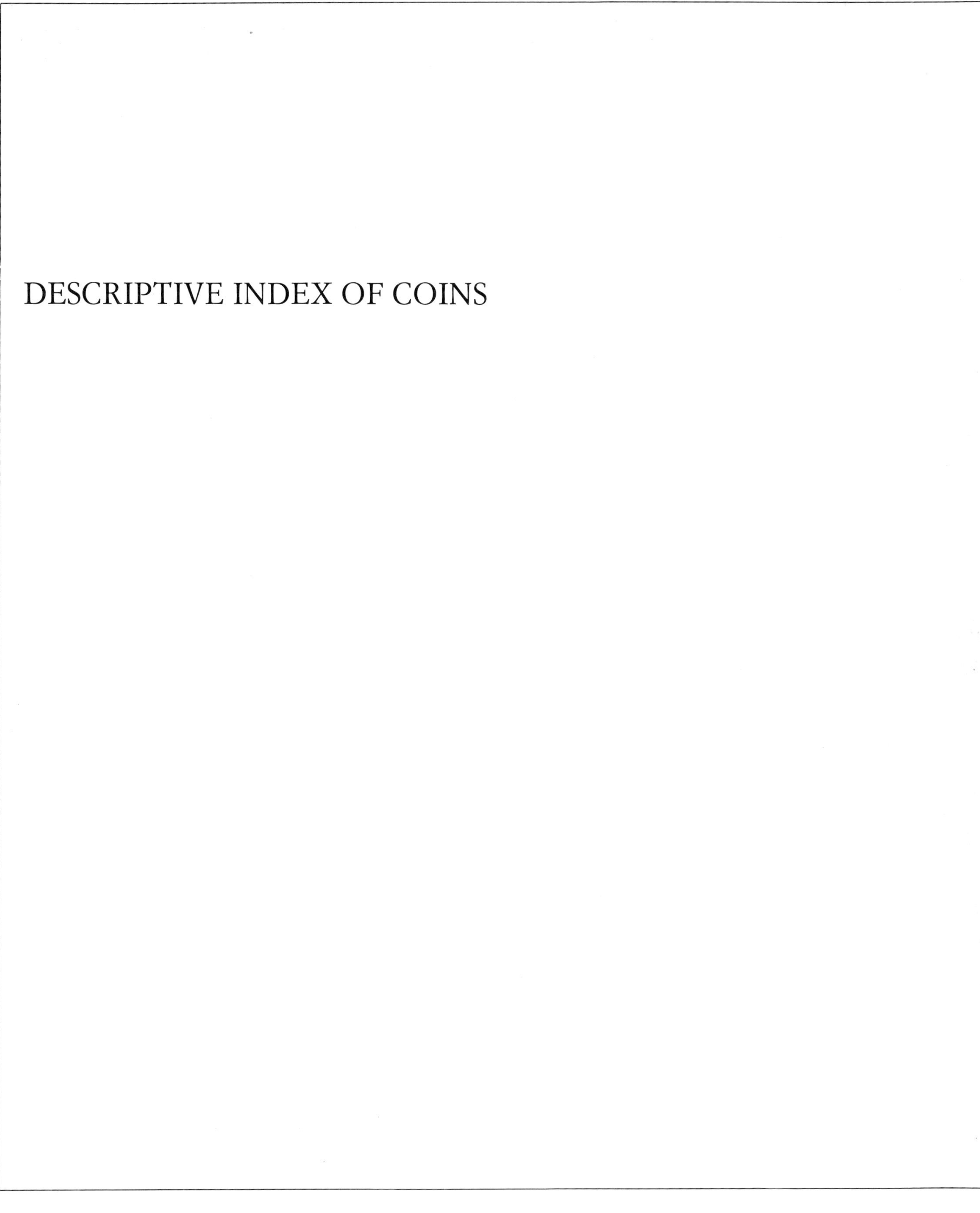

# DESCRIPTIVE INDEX OF COINS

# DESCRIPTIVE INDEX OF COINS

PLATE

I

CLEOPATRA VII.

Bronze coin minted at Alexandria during her reign (52-30 B.C.).

Obverse: no legend. Draped bust of the queen right.

Reverse: ΚΛΕΟΠΑΤΡΑΣ ΒΑΣΙΛΙΣΣΑΣ. Eagle left on a fulmen; in the field at the left a double cornucopia, to the right Π.

*BMC 4/5; Svor. 1871, Plate 63.3. (Private collection).*

---

II and III

OCTAVIA and MARK ANTONY.

Aureus coined probably in the mint at Ephesus about 40 B.C.

Obverse: M·ANTONIUS IMP·III·VIR·R·P·C. Head of Mark Antony right.

Reverse: no legend. Draped bust of Octavia right.

*Grueber II, 499, no number; Sydenham 1196; M. v. Bahrfeldt: "Die Römische Goldmünzenprägung während der Republik und unter Augustus", Halle 1923, 83-85, No. 88. (Berlin, Staatliche Museen, Münzkabinett).*

---

IV

LIVIA.

Dupondius minted at Rome in 22-23 A.D. in the reign of Tiberius.

Obverse: SALUS AUGUSTA. Draped bust of Livia bare-headed, right.

Reverse: TI CAESAR DIVI AUG P M TR POT XXIIII. In the field, S C.

*Cohen 5; RIC 23. (Berlin, Staatliche Museen, Münzkabinett).*

V

LIVIA.

Dupondius coined at Rome in 22-23 A.D. in the reign of Tiberius.

Obverse: IUSTITIA. Draped bust of Livia diademed, right.

Reverse: TI CAESAR DIVI AUG P M TR POT XXIIII. In the field, S C.

*Cohen 4; RIC 22. (Berlin, Staatliche Museen, Münzkabinett).*

---

VI
above

AUGUSTUS.

Denarius coined at Rome about 29-28 B.C.

Obverse: no legend. Head of Octavian, right.

Reverse: CAESAR DIVI F. Partly-draped Venus standing right, seen from the rear, leaning on a column and holding a helmet and a spear. Behind the column, a shield.

*Cohen 62; RIC 26. (Private collection).*

---

VI
below

JULIA.

Bronze theatre ticket.

Obverse: no legend. Draped bust of Julia with crown of grain ears, right.

Reverse: Roman numeral VI surrounded by a border of dots and a crown.

*Compare Cohen under "Tessères", pp. 256, 260. (Private collection).*

---

VII

ANTONIA THE YOUNGER.

Dupondius struck at Rome between 41-54 A.D., in the reign of Claudius.

Obverse: ANTONIA AUGUSTA. Draped bust of Antonia right.

Reverse: TI CLAUDIUS CAESAR AUG P M TR P IMP. Claudius standing draped with head covered and holding a sacrificial ladle to the right. In the field, S C.

*Cohen 6; RIC 82. (Private collection).*

VIII and IX

AGRIPPINA THE ELDER.

Sestertius minted at Rome between 37-41 A.D. in the reign of Caligula.

Obverse: AGRIPPINA M F MAT C CAESARIS AUGUSTI. Draped bust of Agrippina right.

Reverse: S-P-Q-R MEMORIAE AGRIPPINAE. A *carpentum* drawn by two mules, left.

*Cohen 1; RIC 42. (Private collection).*

---

X

CALIGULA.

Sestertius minted at Rome in 37-38 A.D.

Obverse: C CAESAR AUG GERMANICUS PON M TR POT. Laureate head of Caligula left.

Reverse: AGRIPPINA DRUSILLA IULIA. In the exergue, S C. The three sisters of Caligula standing front in the guise of three divinities, Securitas, with a cornucopia resting on a column, Concordia, with a patera and a cornucopia, and Fortuna with a rudder and a cornucopia.

*Cohen 4; RIC 26. (London, British Museum).*

---

XI

MESSALINA.

Bronze coin minted at Nicaea between 41 and 48 A.D. during the reign of Claudius.

Obverse: ΜΕΣΣΑΛΕΙΝΑ ΣΕΒΑΣΤΗ ΝΕΑ ΗΡΑ. Draped bust of Messalina right; before her, two grain ears.

Reverse: Γ ΚΑΔΙΟΣ ΡΟΥΦΟΣ ΑΝΘΥΠΑΤΟΣ. A two-storied temple, below which ΝΕΙΚΑΙΕΩΝ.

*Cohen 1. (Paris, Cabinet des Médailles).*

---

XII

AGRIPPINA and CLAUDIUS.

Aureus coined at Rome between 51 and 54 A.D.

Obverse: TI CLAUD CAESAR AUG GERM P M TRIB POT P P. Laureate head of Claudius right.

Reverse: AGRIPPINAE AUGUSTAE. Draped bust of Agrippina crowned with grain ears, right.

*Cohen 3; RIC 92. (Private collection).*

PLATE

XIII

CLAUDIUS and AGRIPPINA.

Cistophorus coined probably at Ephesus about 50-51 A.D.

Obverse: TI·CLAUD·CAES·AUG·AGRIPP·AUGUSTA. Laureate head of Claudius and draped bust of Agrippina left.

Reverse: DIANA EPHESIA. Statue of Diana of Ephesus.

*Cohen 1; RIC 54. (Private collection).*

---

XIV

AGRIPPINA and NERO.

Didrachm coined at the mint of Caesarea in Cappadocia in 54-55 A.D.

Obverse: NERO CLAUD·DIVI CLAUD·F·CAESAR AUG·GERMANI. Youthful laureate head of Nero right.

Reverse: AGRIPPINA·AUGUSTA·MATER·AUGUSTI. Draped bust of Agrippina right.

*Cohen 1; RIC 11. (Private collection).*

---

XV

AGRIPPINA and NERO.

Aureus minted at Rome in 54 A.D.

Obverse: AGRIPP AUG DIVI CLAUD NERONIS CAES MATER. Confronted draped bust of Agrippina and head of the young Nero.

Reverse: NERONI CLAUD DIVI F CAES AUG GERM IMP TR P. The *corona civica* inside of which EX S C.

*Cohen 6; RIC 9. (London, British Museum).*

---

XVI

NERO and AGRIPPINA.

Denarius minted at Rome in 54-55 A.D.

Obverse: NERO CLAUD DIVI F CAES AUG GERM IMP TR P COS. Head of young Nero and draped bust of Agrippina jugate, right.

Reverse: AGRIPP AUG DIVI CLAUD NERONIS CAES MATER. The deified Augustus and Claudius (?) seated on a quadriga of elephants left. In the field, EX S C.

*Cohen 4; RIC 10. (Private collection).*

---

XVII
above

POPPAEA.

Drachma minted at an unknown mint of Asia Minor after 63 A.D., during the reign of Nero.

Obverse: ΝΕΡΩΝ ΚΑΙΣ[ΑΡ] ΣΕΒΑΣΤΟΣ. Laureate head of Nero right.

Reverse: ΠΟΠΠΑΙΑ [ΝΕΡΩΝΟΣ ΣΕ]ΒΑΣΤΟΥ. Draped bust of Poppaea right.

*Macdonald: "Hunter Collection" p. 732, 13; Jameson 52. (Private collection).*

---

XVII
below

NERO.

Sestertius coined at Lugdunum (Lyons) between 64 and 68 A.D.

Obverse: NERO CLAUD CAESAR AUG GER P M TR P IMP P P. Laureate head of Nero left; below the neck, a globe.

Reverse: DECURSIO. Nero, galloping right with spear, followed by a horseman with a standard. In the field, S C.

*Cohen 84; RIC 128. (Private collection).*

---

XVIII

DOMITILLA.

Denarius coined at Rome in 80-81 A.D. during the reign of Titus.

Obverse: DIVA DOMITILLA AUGUSTA. Draped bust of Domitilla right.

Reverse: FORTUNA AUGUST. Fortune, standing left, holding a rudder and a cornucopia.

*Cohen 3; RIC 71. (Private collection).*

---

XIX

VESPASIAN.

As coined at Rome 74 A.D.

Obverse: IMP CAESAR VESP AUG COS V̄ CENS. Laureate head of Vespasian left.

Reverse: S C. Hope, moving left, holding a flower in her right hand and holding her skirt with her left.

*Cohen 453; RIC 560 b. (Private collection).*

---

XX

JULIA, daughter of TITUS.

Dupondius coined at Rome between 79 and 81 A.D. during the reign of Titus.

Obverse: IULIA IMP·T·AUG F AUGUSTA. Draped bust of Julia right.

Reverse: VESTA (in exergue). Vesta, seated left, holding the palladium and a long sceptre. In the field, S C.

*Cohen 18; RIC 180. (Private collection).*

XXI
above

DOMITIA.

Aureus minted at Rome about 82-83 A.D., during the reign of Domitian.

Obverse: DOMITIA·AUGUSTA·IMP·DOMITIANI. Draped bust of Domitia right.

Reverse: CONCORDIA AUGUST. Peacock right.

*Not in Cohen; RIC 212 B. (Private collection).*

XXI
below

DOMITIAN.

Cistophorus minted in a mint of Asia Minor, perhaps Ephesus, in 80-81 A.D.

Obverse: CAES DIVI F DOMITIANUS COS VII. Laureate head of Domitian right.

Reverse: DIVO VESP. Altar.

*Cohen 95; RIC 75. (Private collection).*

XXII

PLOTINA.

Aureus minted at Rome between 113 and 117 A.D. during the reign of Trajan.

Obverse: PLOTINA·AUG IMP·TRAIANI. Bust of Plotina, draped and diademed, right.

Reverse: CAES AUG GERM DAC·COS VI P P. Vesta, seated left, with the palladium and a long sceptre.

*Cohen 2; RIC 730. (Private collection).*

XXIII

MARCIANA.

Denarius minted at Rome between 114 and 117 approximately A.D., during the reign of Trajan.

Obverse: DIVA·AUGUSTA MARCIANA. Bust, draped and diademed, of Marciana, right.

Reverse: CONSECRATIO. Eagle, with open wings, right, holding a sceptre in its claws.

*Cohen 8; RIC 745. (Private collection).*

XXIV

MATIDIA.

Aureus minted at Rome between 114 and approximately 117 A.D., during the reign of Trajan.

Obverse: MATIDIA·AUG·DIVAE MARCIANAE·F. Diademed and draped bust of Matidia right.

Reverse: PIETAS AUGUST. Matidia, standing front and facing left, holding her hands on the heads of her daughters Sabina and Matidia the Younger.

*Cohen 9; RIC 759. (Private collection).*

XXV

HADRIAN, TRAJAN and PLOTINA.

Aureus minted at Rome between 134 and 138 A.D., during the reign of Hadrian.

Obverse: HADRIANUS AUG COS III P P. Draped bust of Hadrian right.

Reverse: DIVIS·PARENTIBUS. Draped busts of Trajan and Plotina facing; above their heads, two stars.

*Cohen 2; RIC 232 b. (Private collection).*

XXVI

SABINA.

Sestertius minted at Rome between 117 and 136 A.D. during the reign of Hadrian.

Obverse: SABINA AUGUSTA HADRIANI AUG P P. Draped bust of Sabina, right.

Reverse: PIETAS AUG. Pietas, standing front looking left, resting her hands on the heads of a girl and boy. In the field, S C.

*Cohen 52; RIC 1030. (Private collection).*

XXVII
above

SABINA.

Aureus minted at Rome between 117 and 136 A.D. during the reign of Hadrian.

Obverse: SABINA AUGUSTA. Diademed and draped bust of Sabina right.

Reverse: CONCORDIA AUG. Concordia, seated left, holding a patera. At her left, a small statue of Hope.

*Not in Cohen; BMC p. 359, no. 935. (Private collection).*

XXVII
below

HADRIAN.

Aureus coined at Rome between 125 and 128 A.D.

Obverse: HADRIANUS AUGUSTUS. Laureate head of Hadrian right.

Reverse: COS III. Hadrian, mounted right, with his right hand raised.

*Cohen 406 variant; RIC 186; BMC p. 293 no. 429. (Private collection).*

XXVIII
above

FAUSTINA THE ELDER.

Aureus coined at Rome between 141 and 161 A.D., during the reign of Antoninus Pius.

Obverse: DIVA FAUSTINA. Diademed and veiled bust of Faustina left.

Reverse: AUGUSTA. Ceres, standing left, veiled, holding a sceptre and a torch.

*Cohen 98; RIC 356. (Private collection).*

XXVIII
below

ANTONINUS PIUS.

Sestertius minted at Rome between 140 and 144 A.D.

Obverse: ANTONINUS AUG PIUS P P TR P COS III. Laureate head of Antoninus Pius right.

Reverse: APOLLINI AUGUSTO. Apollo standing front, looking left, holding a patera and a lyre. In the field, S C.

*Cohen 62; RIC 598. (Private collection).*

XXIX

FAUSTINA THE ELDER.

Sestertius minted at Rome between 141 and 161 A.D., during the reign of Antoninus Pius.

Obverse: DIVA FAUSTINA. Draped bust of Faustina right.

Reverse: S C. Vesta, standing left, holding a long torch and the palladium.

*Cohen 268; RIC 1151. (Private collection).*

XXX

FAUSTINA THE YOUNGER.

Aureus minted at Rome between about 147 and 161 A.D., during the reign of Antoninus Pius.

Obverse: FAUSTINAE AUG PII AUG FIL. Draped bust of Faustina right.

Reverse: VENERI GENETRICI. Venus, standing left, holding a long sceptre in her left hand.

*Cohen 230 variant; RIC 511 variant (without the fruit in the right hand of Venus). (Private collection).*

XXXI

FAUSTINA THE YOUNGER.

Aureus minted at Rome between 161 and 176 A.D., during the reign of Marcus Aurelius.

Obverse: FAUSTINA AUGUSTA. Draped bust of Faustina right.

Reverse: MATRI MAGNAE. Cybele, seated right between two lions, holding a tympanum.

*Cohen 168; RIC 704. (London, British Museum).*

XXXII
above

MARCUS AURELIUS.

Orichalcum medallion struck at Rome between 145 and 148 A.D. in the reign of Antoninus Pius.

Obverse: AURELIUS CAESAR AUG PII F COS II. Youthful draped bust of Marcus Aurelius right.

Reverse: no legend. Antoninus Pius in military dress, head draped, sacrificing. A servant leads a pig. A short distance behind the altar, another servant holds a plate. Behind the emperor a genius with cornucopia and Phrygian cap. In the background a temple.

*Gnecchi II, 84. (Berlin, Staatliche Museen, Münzkabinett).*

XXXII
below

FAUSTINA THE YOUNGER.

Aureus struck at Rome between 147 and 161 A.D. in the reign of Antoninus Pius.

Obverse: FAUSTINA AUG PII AUG FIL. Draped bust of Faustina left.

Reverse: CONCORDIA. Dove right.

*Cohen 60; RIC 503 b. (Private collection).*

---

XXXIII

LUCILLA.

Aureus minted at Rome between 161 and 180 A.D., during the reign of Marcus Aurelius.

Obverse: LUCILLAE AUG ANTONINI AUG F. Draped bust of Lucilla right.

Reverse: PIETAS. Pietas, draped, standing left beside a flaming altar, raising her right hand and holding an incense box in her left.

*Cohen 49; RIC 774. (Private collection).*

---

XXXIV

CRISPINA.

Aureus minted at Rome between 180 and 185 A.D., during the reign of Commodus.

Obverse: CRISPINA AUGUSTA. Draped bust of Crispina right.

Reverse: PUDICITIA. Pudicitia, veiled, standing left, raising her right hand to veil her face.

*Cohen 29; RIC 285. (Private collection).*

---

XXXV
abovc

CRISPINA.

Sestertius minted at Rome between 180 and 185 A.D., during the reign of Commodus.

Obverse: CRISPINA AUGUSTA. Draped bust of Crispina right.

Reverse: HILARITAS. Hilaritas, standing left, holding a long palm and a cornucopia. In the field, S C.

*Cohen 19; RIC 668. (Private collection).*

---

XXXV
below

COMMODUS.

Sestertius minted at Rome in 192 A.D.

Obverse: L AEL AUREL COMM AUG P FEL. Head of Commodus right wearing a lion's skin.

Reverse: HERCULI ROMANO AUGUSTO S C. Club in a laurel crown.

*Cohen 192; RIC 638. (Private collection).*

---

XXXVI

MANLIA SCANTILLA.

Aureus minted at Rome between 28 March - 1 June, 193 A.D., during the reign of Didius Julianus.

Obverse: MANL SCANTILLA·AUG. Draped bust of Manlia Scantilla right.

Reverse: IUNO·REGINA. Juno, veiled, standing left, holding a patera and a long sceptre; by her feet, a peacock.

*Cohen 1; RIC 7 a. (London, British Museum).*

---

XXXVII

DIDIA CLARA.

Aureus minted at Rome between 28 March - 1 June, 193 A.D., during the reign of Didius Julianus.

Obverse: DIDIA·CLARA·AUG. Draped bust of Didia Clara right.

Reverse: HILAR TEMPOR. Hilaritas, standing left, holding a long palm and a cornucopia.

*Cohen 2; RIC 10. (London, British Museum).*

---

XXXVIII

SEPTIMIUS SEVERUS and JULIA DOMNA.

Aureus minted at Rome in 201 A.D. in the reign of Septimius Severus.

Obverse: ANTONINUS PIUS AUG PON TR P IIII. Bust of the youthful Caracalla, laureate, draped and wearing a breastplate, right.

Reverse: CONCORDIAE AETERNAE. Jugate busts of Septimius Severus, draped and crowned, and Julia Domna, draped and diademed, right; below the bust of Julia Domna, a crescent moon.

*Cohen 1; RIC 52. (Private collection).*

XXXIX

JULIA DOMNA, CARACALLA and GETA.

Aureus minted at Rome after 198 A.D., during the reign of Septimius Severus.

Obverse: IULIA AUGUSTA. Draped bust of Julia Domna, right.

Reverse: AETERNIT IMPERI. Confronted, draped busts of the youthful Caracalla and Geta. Caracalla wears a laurel crown.

*Cohen 1; RIC 540. (Private collection).*

XL and XLI

JULIA DOMNA.

Sestertius minted at Rome between 211 and 217 A.D., during the reign of Caracalla.

Obverse: IULIA PIA FELIX AUG. Draped and diademed bust of Julia Domna, right.

Reverse: VESTA. Vesta, seated left, holding a sacrificial ladle and a long sceptre. In the exergue, S C.

*Cohen 228; RIC 593. (Private collection).*

XLII

PLAUTILLA.

Denarius minted at Rome between 202 and 205 A.D., during the reign of Septimius Severus.

Obverse: PLAUTILLA AUGUSTA. Draped bust of Plautilla right.

Reverse: CONCORDIA AUGG. Concordia, standing left, holding a sceptre and a patera.

*Cohen 1; RIC 363 (b). (Private collection).*

XLIII

CARACALLA.

Sestertius minted at Rome between 210 and 213 A.D.

Obverse: M AUREL ANTONINUS PIUS AUG BRIT. Draped and laureate bust of Caracalla right.

Reverse: SECURITATI·PERPETUAE. Securitas, seated right before an altar, resting her head in her right hand and holding a sceptre in her left. In the exergue, S C.

*Cohen 576 variant (on the obverse legend added* PIUS*); RIC 512 (c). (Private collection).*

XLIV

JULIA MAESA.

Sestertius minted at Rome between 218 and 222 A.D., during the reign of Elagabalus.

Obverse: IULIA MAESA AUGUSTA. Draped and diademed bust of Julia Maesa right.

Reverse: PIETAS AUG. Pietas, standing left before an altar, wreathed and flaming, raising her right arm and holding in her left an incense box. In the field, S C.

*Cohen 31; RIC 414. (Private collection).*

---

XLV
above

JULIA SOAEMIAS.

Denarius minted at Rome between 218 and 222 A.D., during the reign of Elagabalus.

Obverse: IULIA SOAEMIAS AUG. Draped bust of Julia Soaemias right.

Reverse: VENUS CAELESTIS. Venus, diademed, seated left, holding in her hands an apple and a sceptre. By her feet, a child.

*Cohen 14; RIC 243. (Private collection).*

---

XLV
below

ELAGABALUS.

Denarius minted at Rome between 218 and 222 A.D.

Obverse: IMP ANTONINUS PIUS AUG. Laureate draped bust of Elagabalus with horns, right.

Reverse: SUMMUS SACERDOS AUG. Elagabalus standing left, in the act of sacrificing on a tripod, holding in his hands a patera and a branch. In the field, a star.

*Cohen 276; RIC 146. (Private collection).*

---

XLVI

JULIA PAULA.

Denarius minted at Rome between about 219 and 220 A.D., during the reign of Elagabalus.

Obverse: IULIA PAULA AUG. Draped bust of Julia Paula right.

Reverse: CONCORDIA. Concordia, seated left, holding a patera in her right hand. In the field, a star.

*Cohen 6; RIC 211. (Private collection).*

XLVII
above

AQUILIA SEVERA.

Sestertius minted at Rome between 220 and 222 A.D., during the reign of Elagabalus.

Obverse: IULIA AQUILIA SEVERA AUG. Diademed and draped bust of Aquilia Severa right.

Reverse: CONCORDIA. Concordia, standing left by a decorated flaming altar, holding a patera in her right hand and a double cornucopia resting on her left arm. In the field, S C and a star.

*Cohen 4; RIC 390. (Private collection).*

XLVII
below

ANNIA FAUSTINA.

Sestertius coined in Rome about 221 A.D., during the reign of Elagabalus.

Obverse: ANNIA FAUSTINA AUGUSTA. Diademed and draped bust of Annia Faustina right.

Reverse: CONCORDIA. Elagabalus and Annia Faustina standing and shaking hands. In the field, a star; in the exergue, S C.

*Cohen 2; RIC 399. (Berlin, Staatliche Museen, Münzkabinett).*

XLVIII

JULIA MAMAEA.

Bronze medallion struck at Rome in 228 A.D., during the reign of Alexander Severus.

Obverse: IULIA MAMAEA AUGUSTA. Draped, winged bust of Julia Mamaea to right. The Augusta is wearing a diadem decorated with grain ears and on the top of her head has a lotus flower. Behind her neck there appears a crescent moon. In her right hand she holds a cornucopia and in her left a torch ornamented with grain ears.

Reverse: FELICITAS PERPETUA. Mamaea, seated left, holding a sceptre; before her two women are standing; behind her, Felicitas with a caduceus.

*Cohen 15; BMC 537. (London, British Museum).*

XLIX
above

ORBIANA.

Sestertius minted at Rome in 225 A.D., during the reign of Alexander Severus.

Obverse: SALL BARBIA ORBIANA AUG. Draped and diademed bust of Orbiana right.

Reverse: CONCORDIA AUGUSTORUM. Alexander Severus, standing right, holding a book and giving his hand to Orbiana, also standing. In the exergue, S C.

*Cohen 6; RIC 657. (Private collection).*

XLIX below

ALEXANDER SEVERUS.

Denarius minted at Rome in 231 A.D.

Obverse: IMP ALEXANDER PIUS AUG. Laureate, draped bust of Alexander Severus wearing a breastplate to the right.

Reverse: IOVI PROPUGNATORI. Jupiter, nude, his cloak flying in the wind, holding an eagle in his left hand and brandishing a thunderbolt in his right.

*Cohen 83; RIC 238. (Private collection).*

L

PAULINA.

Denarius minted at Rome between 235 and 238 A.D., during the reign of Maximinus Thrax.

Obverse: DIVA PAULINA. Veiled bust of Paulina right.

Reverse: CONSECRATIO. Peacock with tail fanned, standing front.

*Cohen 1; RIC 1. (Private collection).*

LI

TRANQUILLINA.

Antoninianus minted at Rome (compare Kent-Overbeck-Stylow-Hirmer: "Die Römische Münze") or at Antioch (compare RIC) between 241 and 244 A.D. during the reign of Gordian III.

Obverse: SABINIA TRANQUILLINA AUG. Diademed bust of Tranquillina right; behind, a crescent moon.

Reverse: CONCORDIA AUGG. Concordia, seated left, holding in her hands a patera and a double cornucopia.

*Cohen 1; RIC 249. (London, British Museum).*

LII

PHILIP THE ARAB, OTACILIA and PHILIP II.

Bronze medallion struck at Rome in 247 A.D., during the reign of Philip the Arab.

Obverse: CONCORDIA AUGUSTORUM. Draped jugate busts of Philip the Arab laureate and Otacilia diademed, facing a draped bust of their son, Philip II.

Reverse: PONTIFEX MAX TR P IIII COS II P P. A quadriga to the front in which ride Philip and his son. Philip is crowned by Victory holding a palm branch. His son holds his right hand extended. Beside the chariot are two soldiers.

*Cohen 11; Gnecchi II, 10. (London, British Museum).*

LIII
above

ETRUSCILLA.

Antoninianus minted at Rome between 249 and 251 A.D., during the reign of Trajan Decius.

Obverse: HER ETRUSCILLA AUG. Diademed bust of Etruscilla right; behind, a crescent moon.

Reverse: PUDICITIA AUG. Pudicitia, seated left, holding a long sceptre in her left hand, and drawing her veil over her face with her right hand.

*Cohen 19; RIC 59 (b). (Private collection).*

---

LIII
below

CORNELIA SUPERA.

Antoninianus minted in an unknown mint in 253 A.D., during the reign of Aemilianus.

Obverse: COR SUPERA AUG. Diademed bust of Cornelia Supera right; behind, a crescent moon.

Reverse: IUNONI AUG. Juno seated left holding in her right hand a flower and in her left a sceptre.

*Cohen 3; RIC 31. (London, British Museum).*

---

LIV

MARINIANA.

Antoninianus minted at Rome between 254 and 257 A.D., during the reign of Valerian and Gallienus.

Obverse: DIVAE MARINIANAE. Veiled bust of Mariniana right; behind, a crescent moon.

Reverse: CONSECRATIO. A peacock flying right bears Mariniana to heaven.

*Cohen 16; RIC 6. (Munich, Staatliche Münzsammlung).*

---

LV

GALLIENUS and SALONINA.

Silver medallion struck at Rome between about 256 and 258 A.D., during the reign of Valerian and Gallienus.

Obverse: CONCORDIA AUGUSTORUM. Confronted busts of Gallienus, laureate and wearing a breastplate and of Salonina draped and diademed.

Reverse: PIETAS AUGUSTORUM. Confronted busts of Valerian II, son of Gallienus, draped, and of Valerian, father of Gallienus, laureate and wearing a breastplate.

*Not in Cohen; RIC 1; Gnecchi I, 1, plate 26,6. (London, British Museum).*

---

LVI

SEVERINA.

Antoninianus minted at Cyzicus probably in 275 A.D., immediately after the assassination of Aurelian.

Obverse: SEVERINAE AUG. Diademed and draped bust of Severina right; behind, a crescent moon.

Reverse: CONCORDIAE MILITUM. Concordia, standing, facing left, holding two military standards. In the exergue, XXI.

*Cohen 8; RIC 18. (Private collection).*

---

LVII

MAGNIA URBICA.

Aureus coined at Rome in 283 A.D., during the reign of Carinus and Numerian.

Obverse: MAGNIA URBICA AUG. Diademed and draped bust of Magnia Urbica right.

Reverse: VENERI VICTRICI. Venus, standing front, facing right, with her right hand raising her mantle and her left hand holding an apple.

*Cohen 8; RIC 340. (Private collection).*

---

LVIII

GALERIA VALERIA.

Follis minted at Alexandria about 310 A.D., during the reign of Galerius and Licinius.

Obverse: . GAL VALERIA AUG. Draped and diademed bust of Galeria Valeria.

Reverse: VENERI VICTRICI. Venus, standing facing left, raising her veil with her left hand and holding a fruit in her right. In the field, $K^{\Gamma}{}_{P}$; in the exergue, ALE.

*Variant of Cohen 2; RIC 122. (Private collection).*

---

LIX
above

THEODORA.

Follis minted at Trier between 337 and 340 A.D., during the reign of Constantine II, Constantius II and Constans.

Obverse: FL MAX THEODORAE AUG. Laureate and draped bust of Theodora right.

Reverse: PIETAS ROMANA. Pietas (or Theodora) standing front, looking right, holding a child in her arms. In the exergue, TRP.

*Cohen 4. (Private collection).*

---

LIX
below

CONSTANTIUS CHLORUS.

Follis minted at Lugdunum (Lyons) between 303 and 305 A.D.

Obverse: CONSTANTIUS NOB C. Laureate bust of Constantius Chlorus with breastplate, left.

Reverse: GENIO POPULI ROMANI. A half-draped Genius standing looking left; on his head a modius; in his hands a patera and a cornucopia; by his feet a flaming altar. In the field, a star. In the exergue, PLC.

*Cohen 121, RIC 180 a. (Private collection).*

LX

HELENA.

Gold medallion of two solidi, struck at Ticinum (Pavia) about 324-325 A.D., during the reign of Constantine the Great.

Obverse: FL HELENA AUGUSTA. Diademed and draped bust of Helena right.

Reverse: SECURITAS REIPUBLICE. Securitas standing veiled, facing left, holding in her right hand a branch while her left hand supports her dress. In the exergue, SMT.

*Cohen 10; RIC 177. (Paris, Cabinet des Médailles).*

LXI
above

HELENA.

Follis minted at Thessalonica about 318-319 A.D., during the reign of Constantine the Great and Licinius.

Obverse: HELENA N F. Draped bust of Helena right.

Reverse: no legend. A star in a crown.

*Cohen 14; RIC 50. (Private collection).*

LXI
below

CONSTANTINE THE GREAT.

Solidus minted at Antioch in 335-336 A.D.

Obverse: CONSTANTINUS MAX AUG. Diademed and draped bust of Constantine right.

Reverse: VICTORIA CONSTANTINI AUG. Victory moving left holding a trophy in her right hand and palm in her left. In the field VOT XXX; in the exergue, SMAN.

*Cohen 604; RIC 96. (Private collection).*

LXII and LXIII

FAUSTA.

Solidus minted at Ticinum (Pavia) in 324-325 A.D., during the reign of Constantine the Great.

Obverse: FLAV MAX FAUSTA AUG. Draped bust of Fausta right.

Reverse: SALUS REI PUBLICAE. Fausta, standing front, turning her head to the left, holds her sons Constantine II and Constantius in her arms. In the exergue, SMT.

*Cohen 5; RIC 182. (Private collection).*

---

LXIV
above

FLACCILLA.

Majorina struck at Antioch between 383 and 385 A.D., during the reign of Theodosius I.

Obverse: AEL FLACCILLA AUG. Diademed and draped bust of Flaccilla right.

Reverse: SALUS REIPUBLICAE. Flaccilla, standing front, looking right and holding a scroll between her hands. In the exergue, ANTЄ.

*Cohen 6; RIC 54. (Private collection).*

---

LXIV
below

THEODOSIUS I.

Solidus minted at Constantinople between 383 and 388 A.D.

Obverse: D N THEODOSIUS P F AUG. Diademed and draped bust of Theodosius with breastplate, right.

Reverse: CONCORDIA AUGGGΔ. Constantinople helmeted, seated on a throne ornamented with two lions' heads, looking right and placing a foot on the prow of a ship and holding a spear and a shield on which VOT V MUL X. In the exergue, CONOB.

*Cohen 10; RIC 70 (b). (Private collection).*

---

LXV

GALLA PLACIDIA.

Solidus minted at an Italian mint in 443 A.D. during the reign of Valentinian III.

Obverse: GALLA PLACIDIA AUG. Draped and diademed bust of Galla Placidia right; from above a heavenly hand descends to crown her.

Reverse: IMP XXXXII COS XVII P P. Rome, seated left, holding an orb topped with a cross and a sceptre, her right foot resting on the prow of a ship. In the field, a star; in the exergue, COMOB.

*Variant of Cohen 2 (*AUG *lacking in the obverse legend). (Private collection).*

---

LXVI and LXVII

HONORIA.

Solidus minted at Ravenna between 425 and 433 A.D., during the reign of Valentinian III (regency of Galla Placidia).

Obverse: D N IUST GRAT HONORIA P F AUG. Diademed and draped bust of Honoria right; from on high a heavenly hand descends to crown her.

Reverse: BONO REIPUBLICAE. Victory, standing left, holds a cross; above, a star; in the field, R V, in the exergue, COMOB.

*Cohen 1. (Private collection).*

---

LXVIII

AELIA EUDOXIA.

Tremissis minted at Constantinople between 400 and 404 A.D., during the reign of Arcadius.

Obverse: AEL EUDOXIA AUG. Diademed and draped bust of Aelia Eudoxia right.

Reverse: a cross enclosed in a crown. In the exergue, CON.

*Ratto 140 variant* (CONOB *for* CON); *Tolstoi 143. (London, British Museum).*

---

LXIX
above

PULCHERIA.

Solidus minted at Constantinople between 414 and 453 A.D., during the reign of Theodosius II or of Marcianus.

Obverse: AEL PULCHERIA AUG. Draped and diademed bust of Pulcheria right; from on high, a heavenly hand descends to crown her.

Reverse: SALUS REIPUBLICAE. Victory, seated right, tracing the monogram of Christ on a shield resting on her knees. In the field, a star; in the exergue, CONOB.

*Ratto 233; Sabatier 2; Tolstoi 31. (Private collection).*

---

LXIX
below

AELIA EUDOCIA.

Solidus minted at Constantinople about 422 A.D. during the reign of Theodosius II.

Obverse: AEL EUDOCIA AUG. Diademed and draped bust of Aelia Eudocia right; from above, a heavenly hand descends to crown her.

Reverse: VOT XX MULT XXX. Victory, standing, looking left, holding in her right hand a long cross. In the field above, a star; in the exergue, CONOB.

*Ratto 202; Sabatier 1; Tolstoi 90. (London, British Museum).*

---

LXX and LXXI

LICINIA EUDOXIA.

Solidus minted at Ravenna between 439 and 455 A.D., during the reign of Valentinian III.

Obverse: LICINIA EUDOXIA P F AUG. Draped bust of Licinia Eudoxia front, her head adorned with a crown from which fall long strings of pearls. On the crown, a cross.

Reverse: SALUS REIPUBLICAE. Licinia Eudoxia seated on a throne front, holding an orb topped with a cross and a long cross. In the field R V; in the exergue, COMOB.

*Cohen 1. (Private collection).*

Cleopatra VII, born in 69 B.C., queen of Egypt from 51 to 30 B.C., mistress of Caesar and Mark Antony.
Bronze coin minted at Alexandria.

Octavia (died in 11 B.C.), the meek elder sister of Octavian, married in 40 B.C. to Mark Antony.
Aureus (reverse).

The triumvir Mark Antony (82-30 B.C.). Splendid portrait on the obverse of the aureus illustrated in Plate II.

Augustus, born in 63 B.C. and emperor from 31 B.C. to 14 A.D.
Denarius.

Julia (39 B.C.-14 A.D.), only daughter of Augustus, exiled by her father for moral turpitude.
Theatre ticket in bronze.

Antonia the Younger (36 B. C.-37 A.D.), daughter of Octavia and Mark Antony, mother of the emperor Claudius. Excellent posthumous portrait of the time of Claudius.
Dupondius.

Agrippina the Elder (ca. 14 B. C.-33 A.D.), daughter of Julia and Marcus Agrippa, wife of Germanicus and mother of the emperor Caligula. Posthumous portrait ordered by Caligula to commemorate his mother who had tragically died in exile. Sestertius (obverse).

The *carpentum,* the vehicle reserved for the use of the women of the imperial family in the city. Reverse of the sestertius illustrated in Plate VIII.

Agrippina the Younger (15-59 A.D.), Drusilla (17-38 A.D.), and Julia Livilla (18-41 A.D.), daughters of Germanicus and Agrippina the Elder, and younger sisters of the emperor Caligula, shown in the guise of Securitas, Concordia and Fortuna on one of the first coins of the reign of Caligula.
Sestertius (reverse).

Caligula, emperor from 37 to 41 A.D., portrait on the obverse of the same coin.

The young and corrupt Messalina, perhaps born in 25 A.D., died in 48 A.D., great-granddaughter of Octavia and the third wife of the emperor Claudius.
Bronze coin minted at Nicaea.

Agrippina the Younger (15-59 A.D.), daughter of Germanicus and Agrippina the Elder, the fourth wife of the emperor Claudius and the mother of Nero.
Aureus (reverse).

Claudius, son of Drusus and Antonia the Younger, emperor from 41 to 54 A.D. Portrait on the obverse of the same coin.

The aged emperor Claudius and his last wife Agrippina the Younger.
Cistophorus.

A powerful and realistic portrait of Agrippina the Younger, mother of the emperor Nero.
Didrachm issued at an eastern mint.

Agrippina the Younger and the young Nero: portraits made during the first year of his rule, at the time of Agrippina's greatest ascendancy.
Aureus (obverse).

The reverse of the same coin with the legend EX S C, showing the temporary authority exercised by the senate in the first part of Nero's reign, when the young emperor was still a minor and thus under guardianship.

The young Nero and Agrippina represented on a coin minted between 54 and 55 A.D. The titles of the Augusta no longer appear on the obverse but are relegated to a secondary position on the reverse of the coin. This is the first sign of the decline of Agrippina's power. Denarius.

Poppaea, probably born in 31 A.D., died in 65 A.D., the fascinating second wife of Nero and the architect of Agrippina's fall. Drachm from an eastern mint.

A powerful portrait of Nero, emperor from 54 to 68 A.D. Sestertius.

Domitilla (died before 69 A.D.), wife of Vespasian, represented on a coin struck in her memory by her son Titus.
Denarius.

Vespasian, emperor from 69 to
79 A.D.
As.

Julia (died in 91 A.D.), daughter of the emperor Titus and mistress of her uncle, the emperor Domitian, shown as an adolescent on a coin of the period of Titus.
Dupondius.

A crude portrait of Domitia (died about 140 A.D.), wife of the emperor Domitian.
Aureus.

Domitian, emperor from 81 to 96 A.D.
Cistophorus.

Plotina (70-121 A.D.), wife of the emperor Trajan, faithful friend and counselor of her adopted son, the future emperor Hadrian.
Aureus.

Marciana (born before 53, died about 114 A.D.), beloved sister of the emperor Trajan, in a portrait struck shortly after her death.
Denarius.

Matidia (died 119 A.D.), daughter of Marciana and niece of the emperor Trajan, shown with the complicated and artificial hairstyle of her time also seen in the preceding coin.
Aureus.

The emperor Trajan and his wife Plotina, shown *post mortem* on a coin issued by Hadrian, their adopted son.
Aureus (reverse).

On the obverse of the same coin, an exceptional youthful portrait of Hadrian, emperor from 117 to 138 A.D.

Sabina (died 136 A.D.), daughter of Matidia and wife of the emperor Hadrian, in a cursory youthful portrait.
Sestertius.

Another portrait of Sabina in her maturity.
Aureus.

A splendid portrait of the emperor Hadrian in middle life.
Aureus.

Faustina the Elder (105-140 A.D.), wife of the emperor Antoninus Pius, shown with her head veiled on a coin issued shortly after her death.
Aureus.

Antoninus Pius, emperor from 138 to 161 A.D.
Sestertius.

Another fine posthumous portrait of Faustina the Elder. Sestertius.

Faustina the Younger (130-175 A.D.), daughter of Antoninus Pius and Faustina the Elder and wife of Marcus Aurelius, in a youthful portrait of the time of Antoninus Pius.
Aureus (obverse).

The representation of Venus Genetrix on the reverse of the same coin makes reference to the children presented by Faustina to her husband, the future emperor Marcus Aurelius.

Another portrait, with elaborate hairstyle, of Faustina the Younger, wife of the emperor Marcus Aurelius.
Aureus.

Marcus Aurelius, emperor from 161 to 180 A.D., in a thoughtful youthful portrait. Orichalcum medallion.

Faustina the Younger, shown on a coin belonging to the reign of her father Antoninus Pius. Aureus.

Lucilla (148-182 A.D.), daughter of Marcus Aurelius and Faustina the Younger. The sister and enemy of Commodus is here shown on a coin of the reign of Marcus Aurelius.
Aureus.

Crispina (died after 187 A.D.), beautiful and faithless wife of the emperor Commodus, in a portrait of exceptional beauty. Aureus.

Another thoughtful expression of Crispina.
Sestertius.

Commodus, emperor from 180 to 192 A.D., portrayed as "The Roman Hercules", his hair covered by a lion's skin.
Sestertius.

Manlia Scantilla, wife of Didius Julianus, emperor from 28 March to 1 June, 193 A.D. Aureus.

Didia Clara, daughter of the emperor Didius Julianus.
Aureus.

The emperor Septimius Severus and his wife Julia Domna (died 217 A.D.), daughter of Julius Bassianus, priest of the Sun at Emesa.
Aureus.

Julia Domna, her hair done according to the complicated style of the period, on a coin of the reign of Septimius Severus. Aureus (obverse).

The portraits of Caracalla and Geta as children symbolize on the reverse of the same coin the dynastic continuity assured by the two sons of Septimius Severus and Julia Domna.

Another powerful portrait of Julia Domna in later life. Sestertius (obverse).

The figure of Vesta which appears on the reverse of the sestertius shown in Plate XL is one common to reverses of many coins issued in the name of the Augustae in the time of the Antonines and the Severi. The figure of the goddess is an allegorical compliment to the feminine virtues of the Augusta herself.

Plautilla (died in 211), daughter of Plautianus, powerful praetorian prefect of Septimius Severus. The unhappy wife of the young Caracalla is shown on a coin of the reign of Septimius Severus.
Denarius.

Caracalla, emperor from 211 to 217 A.D., in a portrait which expresses the ferocity of his character.
Sestertius.

Julia Maesa (died in 226 A.D.), sister of Julia Domna and grandmother of the emperors Elagabalus and Alexander Severus, shown on a coin issued during the reign of Elagabalus. Sestertius.

The hard and unpleasant face of Julia Soaemias (died 222 A.D.), daughter of Julia Maesa and mother of Elagabalus.
Denarius.

The youthful priest of the Sun, Elagabalus, emperor from 218 to 222 A.D.
Denarius.

Julia Paula, the first unfortunate
wife of Elagabalus.
Denarius.

Aquilia Severa, the young Vestal virgin, second wife of Elagabalus, in a fine portrait shadowed by melancholy.
Sestertius.

Annia Faustina, third wife of Elagabalus. This is the most summary of the portraits of the three wives of the mad emperor.
Sestertius.

Julia Mamaea (died in 235 A.D.), daughter of Julia Maesa and mother of the emperor Alexander Severus. In this curious portrait the Augusta is given the attributes of various female divinities.
Bronze medallion.

Orbiana, wife of the emperor Alexander Severus, shown in the brief moment of her good fortune at court.
Sestertius.

Alexander Severus, the young and weak emperor, raised to the throne in 222 A.D. and assassinated with his mother in 235 A.D.
Denarius.

Paulina, the wife of Maximinus Thrax, emperor from 235 to 238 A.D., shown veiled on a coin issued after her death.
Denarius (obverse).

The peacock, shown on the reverse of the same coin, was Juno's sacred bird. This image and the legend CONSECRATIO celebrate the deification of the dead empress.

Tranquillina, wife of Gordian III, emperor from 238 to 244 A.D. Behind the bust one sees a crescent moon as a sign of value. Antoninianus.

Philip the Arab (emperor from 244 to 249 A.D.), with his wife, Otacilia Severa, and their son, in a fine family portrait. The legend CONCORDIA AUGUSTORUM celebrates the perfect harmony between the members of the imperial family.
Bronze medallion.

Etruscilla (died perhaps in 251 A.D.), wife of the most implacable persecutor of the Christians, Trajan Decius, emperor from 249 to 251 A.D.
Antoninianus.

Cornelia Supera. Portrait done during the brief reign of her husband Aemilianus, emperor from May to September (?) of 253 A.D.
Antoninianus.

Mariniana (died in 254 A.D.): veiled portrait on a coin issued a short time after her death by her husband Valerian, emperor from 253 to 260 A.D. Antoninianus.

Gallienus, son of Mariniana and Valerian and emperor from 253 to 268 A.D., shown with his wife, Salonina, on a medallion celebrating the marital happiness of the Augusti.
Silver medallion.

Severina, wife of Aurelian, emperor from 270 to 275 A.D. The elegant hairstyle is a strange contrast to the rough, hard face of this Augusta.
Antoninianus.

Magnia Urbica, obscure wife of Carinus, emperor from 283 to 285 A.D.
Aureus.

Galeria Valeria (died in 314 A.D.), daughter of the great Diocletian and wife of Galerius, emperor from 305 to 311 A.D. The portrait of this unhappy Augusta is a magnificent example of the coin style of the Tetrarchy.
Follis.

Theodora (died before 337 A.D.), step-daughter of the emperor Maximian and wife of Constantius Chlorus, emperor from 305 to 306 A.D.
Follis.

The Illyrian general Constantius Chlorus, Caesar from 293 to 305, Augustus from 305 to 306 A.D.
Follis.

Helena, born about 248 and died in 328 A.D., mistress of Constantius Chlorus and mother of the emperor Constantine, in a courtly and refined portrait. Gold medallion of two solidi.

Another, more realistic portrait of Helena.
Follis.

Constantine the Great, emperor from 311 to 337 A.D. The family resemblance between the emperor and his mother Helena is evident in this fine coin.
Solidus.

Fausta (about 298-326 A.D.), daughter of Maximian and wife of the emperor Constantine, in an elegant portrait in which the soft mass of the hair crowns a completely depersonalized face. Solidus (obverse).

On the reverse of the solidus shown in Plate LXII, Fausta is represented holding her two elder sons, Constantine II and Constantius, in her arms. The legend is SALUS REI PUBLICAE. Both the representation and the legend clearly display dynastic propaganda.

Aelia Flaccilla (died in 385 A.D.), the obscure wife of the emperor Theodosius I.
Majorina.

Theodosius I, the Great, emperor from 379 to 395 A.D.
Solidus.

Galla Placidia, born about 390, died in 450 A.D., wife of the Gothic king Athaulf and later of the general Constantius, mother of Valentinian III, emperor of the West from 425 to 455 A.D. Solidus.

Honoria, born in 417, died about 454 A.D., the unhappy daughter of Constantius and Galla Placidia and the betrothed of Attila.
Solidus (obverse).

On the reverse of the solidus of Plate LXVI, Victory, a typical pagan figure, hold the cross of Christ.

Aelia Eudoxia (died in 404 A.D.), wife of Arcadius, emperor of the East from 395 to 408 A.D. This splendid portrait shows the aristocratic beauty of the enemy of St. John Chrysostom.
Tremissis.

Pulcheria (399-453 A.D.), daughter of Arcadius and Aelia Eudoxia. The pious and intelligent sister of the emperor Theodosius II became later the wife of Marcianus, emperor of the East from 450 to 457 A.D.
Solidus.

Eudocia (Athenais), born a pagan about 400 in Athens, died a Christian about 460 in Jerusalem, wife of Theodosius II, emperor of the East from 408 to 450 A.D.
Solidus.

Licinia Eudoxia, born in 422, died after 462, daughter of Theodosius II and Eudocia, wife of Valentinian III, emperor of the West from 425 to 455 A.D. Solidus (obverse).

Licinia Eudoxia enthroned on the reverse of the solidus illustrated in Plate LXX. Both sides of this coin are already executed in an exquisitely Byzantine style.

**Edizioni Arte e Moneta, viale Vittorio Veneto 6 - 20124 Milan (Italy)**
Printed by I.G.D.A. - Officine Grafiche - Novara.

The photographs were provided by Hirmer Verlag, Munich with the exception of those reproduced on plates I, VI (below), VII, XII, XIV, XVII (below), XXIII, XXIV, XXVI, XXVII (above), XXVIII (above), XXX (below), XXXII (below), XXXIII, XXXV (above), XLII, XLIV, XLV (below), XLVII (above), LIII (above), LVI, LVII, LVIII, LIX, LXI (below), LXII, LXIII, LXIV, LXV, LXVI, LXVII, LXIX (above), LXX and LXXI which were executed by Elio Ventura (Studio Fotografico Aprile, Milan). The photograph illustrated on plate XI and those illustrated on plates XVI and XVIII were provided respectively by the Cabinet des Médailles, Paris, and Bank Leu, Zurich. The location of the coins illustrated is given in the « Descriptive Index of Coins ».